C000060917

SINGLE FIGURE
GOLFER

SINGLE FIGURE GOLFER

Peter Smith

The Crowood Press

First published in 1995 by
The Crowood Press Ltd
Ramsbury, Marlborough
Wiltshire SN8 2HR

British Library Cataloguing-in-Publication Data
A catalogue record for this book is available from the British
Library

ISBN 1 85223 913 1

Designed by MasterClass Design Services
Birmingham B36 9TB
Photographs by Charles Beattie

Printed and bound in Great Britain by Redwood Books, Trowbridge
Wiltshire

Contents

Introduction

IT MUST BE the aim of every golfer to get round the course in level par, or better. In reality few golfers will achieve this on a regular basis: even professional golfers don't always beat par as a visit to any Tour event will show you; the number who fail to beat par might actually surprise you. For the club golfer level par might be just out of reach on a regular basis although there will be many times when you come tantalizingly close to it. What a good golfer will do is ensure that his or her scores are regularly in the mid- to upper 70s or low 80s, proving that he or she is a true single figure golfer.

This book is written for those who really want to achieve this. It contains help for those who may not yet be in single figures but have the ability and determination to do so, as well as those who have achieved, or are very close to a single figure handicap now. Not only does it look at the technique needed to make the shots count, but it also explains how to choose the right shot at the right time;

how you can win; and how you can think your way to a low score. Some essential practice routines are included.

For those of you who really want to play in single figures, this book is a vital necessity.

I must apologize to any left-handed golfers for not having the space to reverse all the directions; I am sure you will understand and can only refer you to my book *Left Handed Golfer*, published in 1993.

Finally, a few words of thanks to those without whose help this book could not have happened. The golf clubs and bag come from **Mizuno,** who make the best golf clubs I have ever used; **Glenmuir** continue to supply my clothing as they have done for years; the extremely comfortable shoes come from **Cotswold Shoes,** and the photographs were taken by Charles Beattie at **Carvoeiro** Golf Club in the Algarve; my thanks to Stuart Woodman, the Director of Golf, and his team for their very kind hospitality.

1 Fine Tuning

EVERYONE hates reading about the grip and stance, particularly those who have been playing golf for some time. However, this short chapter is the most important in the book, for without the good foundation of a sound grip and set-up, you will not be able to build a solid and lasting swing. Go to any professional and the first thing they will look at will be the set-up and grip. Even the very top teachers like David Leadbetter, with a champion golfer, will look first at the foundations for the majority of problems in golf are caused by an incorrect set-up and grip.

Good players have learnt how to grip the club correctly, how to stand and how to aim, yet for a variety of reasons they sometimes slip into bad habits, getting very slightly out of kilter. It's the same with a racing car: occasionally it needs fine tuning and so it is with the grip, stance and aim.

THE GRIP

There is no such thing as a perfect grip. Everyone is different in build and the way they swing the club. There are, though, a few vital fundamentals. Whether your grip is strong, weak or neutral, your hands must work together as a single unit. The best grip is the overlapping grip popularized by Harry Vardon almost a century ago. For players with small fingers the ten-finger grip might prove suitable, but do try to avoid the interlocking grip used by Jack Nicklaus. Although it worked for him most professionals will tell you that it is the worst, causing more problems of independent hand movement than any other grip. It is horrible so avoid it. If you use it, change it.

You will know the Vardon grip well, but there are just a couple of little points to check and re-check regularly.

Make sure the 'V's point to the same place.

It does not matter if that is to the right shoulder (left for left-handers) or the chin, but they must be together. Having a strong grip is no problem, but don't let your hands turn too far to the right or you will have problems squaring the clubface at impact. If the 'V's point outside the right shoulder start again, practising taking the grip until you feel comfortable with it. Get a PGA professional to check it for you if it still causes you problems. If the grip is too strong and you hit straight shots it will mean you are compensating with other faults.

The stronger grip is more common than one that is too weak so if you feel your grip is slowly turning further right, move the opposite way, almost to the point where you only show one knuckle on the left hand. That will almost guarantee that you cannot close the clubface through impact. Learn to get this right rather than trying to compensate in any other way during the swing. Keep your hands 'tied' together.

Ensure that the 'V's formed by the joint of the thumb and forefinger point to the same place.

Many problems in the swing can be caused by the grip coming loose at the top of the backswing. Does yours?

You can check this yourself. Next time you are practising, take your normal grip, hit a shot and then, *without moving your hands off the club,* address a second ball. Is the clubface still perfectly square to the ball? If it is, well done, your grip has not moved on the club.

I would imagine that for most people, however, the clubface will not be perfectly square but will be aiming very slightly left of target for the better players. It will need to be re-gripped and squared up.

What is going wrong? Basically, this happens because you let go of the club at the top of the backswing. You will see the effect of this in slightly hooked shots and in extra wear on the golf glove as the club turns in the hands. You might need to grip slightly tighter with the middle fingers of the *right* hand, though do avoid trying to crush the club as that will deprive you of feeling in the hands.

It used to be thought that the right-hand grip should be fairly light, but we are coming to realize that this is not so. When you write you do so with your dominant hand. If you throw a ball you do so with your dominant hand. When you play golf it surely must be correct to do so with your dominant hand in control.

You might also need to slide the hands closer together. With your normal grip in position, try to slide the right hand up the club a little more, squeezing it into the left hand. Make sure the thumb pad on the right hand completely covers the left thumb. It is only a very slight difference yet that is all that is needed.

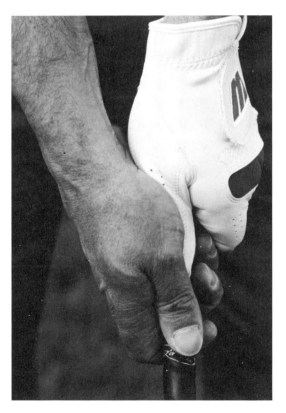

Ensure your hands are firmly 'tied' together – slide them as close as they will go.

Try a very slight alteration to find what works best for you. Remember, it is *your* grip that counts, not anyone else's. On the course, check your grip every few shots. Get into the habit of doing this, though make it a quick check; never stand there fiddling with the grip. If it feels wrong, move away, put the club back in the bag and start all over again. Don't be pressurized into making a swing until you are happy with the set-up. You only get one chance.

A lever swings fastest at 90 degrees to its axis, but you must feel and look comfortable rather than stretching for the ball.

STANCE

Your stance or posture over the ball is something individual. I can't tell you to stand like Faldo, Els or Woosnam, because you might not have their stature. I don't, so I don't try to look like them. What any professional coach wants to see is a good spine angle relative to the club shaft, and good balance.

A lever will fly fastest when it is at 90 degrees to its axis. The club is a lever, the spine is the axis, so ideally your club should be at a 90 degree angle to your spine. Yours might not be, so try to adjust your stance to being closer to 90 degrees than it is now. Do beware, however, of having the ball too far from you, as this will make you stretch and become unbalanced.

As you hold the club ensure that your right elbow is not too far forward. If, as you look down, your right elbow is further forward than your left, you have the wrong stance: the right elbow should be behind the left. Have your legs slightly flexed, and be poised, looking, and feeling, like an athlete. If you can stay in control of your balance as you turn and swing you are probably correctly poised at address.

AIM

The ball will go where you aim it, so make sure that the clubface is square to the target. Most professionals approach the ball from behind, looking down the line to the target and selecting a second 'target' a few feet ahead of the ball to align the clubface with. You can probably check that the clubface is square to the target with either extra clubs or tape on the ground; you could also use a tee-peg stuck to the clubface (of a fairly straight-faced club like a 5-iron) with Blu-tak or something similar.

It's easier to line up with something a couple of feet away than something 200 yards (180 metres) away. Do this every time you hit a shot, even in practice. Get into the habit, because the habits you form on the practice range you take with you onto the golf course.

You should also check that your feet are correctly aligned, though many players like to have their left foot very slightly splayed out, which will mean that the toes on the left foot are further back than those of the right foot. Check it by having your heels against a club laid parallel to the ball-to-target line.

Finally, check your body aim,

or rather have someone check it for you as it is very difficult to check it yourself.What will need assistance is the check on the alignment of your shoulders because it is almost impossible to check for yourself that your shoulders are correctly aligned.

Get a friend or professional to watch you line up as you address the ball. By having someone to help re-align your shoulders every time you will get to feel the correct position. Do it twenty times or more and then check it again a few days later. Keep checking and

Ask a friend to check your shoulder aim by holding a club across your chest parallel to the ball-to-target line.

re-checking it. If you play non-competitive games with a friend, have him or her check it for you as often as possible on the course. Get into good habits when you practise, so that they become second nature when you are on the course.

Check your grip, set-up and aim regularly. Never assume that it will stay the same all the time. It will alter every time you change your clothes, so just take a second or two to check. It might save you several shots and maybe a few minutes looking for a lost ball!

The ball will go where you aim it; take your time aiming.

2 Equipment

GOLF CLUBS

DO YOUR shoes fit you, or are you wearing a pair two sizes too big? A stupid question, really, but you'd be amazed at the number of golfers whose golf clubs don't fit them. Do yours?

The clubs you use have probably been with you for some time and you have come to regard them (well, most of the time!) as friends. But unlike some friends who might have the odd idiosyncrasy, these you can have altered. The main problem with golf clubs is that they are normally bought as standard sets, but since not everyone is the same height, having shafts of a standard length is not ideal; though it would not really be practicable for the manufacturers to make them to measure for everyone.

The Length of a Club

Check the length of your clubs, or rather go to a professional with a fitting centre to have them checked. Tall players might need a one-inch plug fitted to the top of the shafts to lengthen the clubs, as some tour players have had done. Short players might need an inch cut off the top of the shaft, which is quite possible although it very slightly stiffens the shaft. All clubs, including putters and drivers, can have their shafts lengthened or shortened and it costs very little.

The Lie of a Club

The main problem is the lie and, to an extent, the loft of the clubs. Getting the lie correct is vital or it becomes impossible to catch the ball perfectly square. Most golf clubs these days have slightly rounded soles and it used to be assumed that if you could slide an old penny (now a 10p piece) under the toe of the club the lie was about correct. However, science has now arrived in golf and you can have the lie of your clubs checked with the aid of a computer! You can also do a little check for yourself: go to a driving range with those black mats and hit half-a-dozen shots off the mat rather than off the artificial 'grass'. The black streaks on the bottom of the club should be in the middle. If they are towards the toe, the clubs are too flat; if towards the heel, too upright.

Don't just check one club, of course, but try at least four or five and preferably all of them, as they are not always made standard in the factory. The lie should be checked at least every year as it is possible to knock the clubs out of kilter in the normal process of playing golf, particularly if playing off hard ground.

The Loft of a Club

The loft is also something you can have altered and will make quite a difference to your game. I always used to find that I was struggling for distance with standard clubs so I had mine strengthened by two degrees. Normally the difference between each club is about four degrees so in effect I added half a club to each shot, which I find ideal. With the peripherally weighted clubs these days, which have a lower centre of gravity and thus hit the ball higher, you might find that you want slightly more penetration with your shots, rather than height. Strengthening the loft by a degree or two might work for you as well, though have one club changed first to see.

Choosing Clubs

The clubs I use are Mizuno TP18 as I prefer the shape of a blade to that of peripherally weighted clubs, but it is a matter of personal choice, most players these days using the cavity-back clubs which help many players get the ball airborne easier and, to an extent, keep it on line better. Although I would never suggest you chop and change (even if you could afford to) I do think it worth while to try a new set of clubs now and again; the vast majority of PGA professionals will allow you to use a trial set on the course. Never buy a new set based on half-a-dozen shots hit off a mat into a net in a high street or club pro-shop; you'd never consider buying a new car without taking it for a test drive; golf clubs are not cheap either.

Types of shaft

Two other parts of the golf club are vital: the shaft and the grip.

Shafts come in a variety of flex strengths, with some of the top tour professionals playing with very stiff shafts; other players need whippier shafts to help them achieve sufficient clubhead speed.

Stiffer shafts do help you to hit the ball better, but only if you have a sufficiently powerful swing to square the clubhead at impact. A shaft too stiff for your swing could make you hit more from the shoulders, causing poor shots. Don't get any macho ideas about better players only using stiffer shafts - several European Tour players use regular shafts. When you buy a set of clubs the supplier will provide whichever shafts you want, for no extra cost.

Much has been written about graphite shafts and undoubtedly these will become more and more popular; they have improved dramatically since they were first introduced. Today's graphite (and other material such as boron) shafts are excellent and come in varying degrees of flex. They normally help the player with a slower swing although the very stiff graphite shafts are being used by some Tour players, though so far only the drivers. Without any doubt, within a few years, graphite-shafted irons will be a regular feature in tournament golf.

Grips

Club grips are basically either cord or wrap-round and what you choose is a matter of personal choice. I prefer Tour wraps as they give a softer feel, though the cord grips are better in wet weather.

You must keep the grips clean and dry during your game of golf, and they should be washed in warm, soapy water very regularly, using a soft nail-brush to clear away any ingrained dirt or grease. They should also be changed regularly (a very inexpensive operation which almost any PGA professional will undertake) as playing with worn grips is like driving a car with bald tyres. Once they become a little shiny is the time to change them, but I would suggest at least once a year, more if you play very regularly.

Care of Equipment

Looking after your clubs is, of course, vital. The biggest problem is that they get dirty, with mud caked into the grooves. Sadly, many players don't clean this out, which inevitably affects their performance and in particular the amount of backspin they can get on a shot. After each shot wipe the clubface clean, making sure there is no dirt or grass in the grooves. When you get home, or to the clubhouse if that is where you store your clubs, clean them properly, using a soft nail-brush to clean the grooves. You can also buy small regrooving tools that dig into the metal and re-shape the grooves, but make sure they remain within the regulations.

It is just as important to keep the grips clean and in good condition. On the course they get dirty with sweat and grease from your hands; some players also drop them on the grass, so sap gets on them. Rain affects them and if they sit in the car boot they pick up dust and dirt. It may be too much to ask that you wash them every week but that is the ideal; it probably takes ten minutes and is time well worth spending. Wash them in warm, soapy water (washing-up liquid), wipe them dry and then leave them in a warm, airy place to dry thoroughly. Look after your golf clubs and they will look after you.

Finally, clean and dry your golf shoes properly, using good leather polish. The spikes will require changing from time to time; never let them wear down too far.

If you want to be a serious golfer you must act like one.

GOLF BALLS

Golf balls do make a difference and any decent player really should be playing with a balata ball which, being softer, is easier to control. The softer the ball the more time it spends in contact with the clubface during impact, and the better the clubface can control its direction. A softer ball also spreads out more over the clubface at impact, leaving a larger 'footprint' on the clubface. I use Titleist tour wound 100 balata balls, though there is a lot of confusion over ball pressure. To be honest, there is very little difference as the balls are all manufactured together and are sorted according to a rather unscientific formula.

There is also confusion over the length of time a balata ball will last; it is not necessary, as some tour professionals do, to change it every few holes. In reality they are fine as long as they do not become too scratched or scored. I strongly recommend, however, that you use a new golf ball as often as necessary, at least in competitive golf. I would never play with a balata ball in competitive golf for more than nine holes, personally.

Golf balls do react to air

temperature, flying further in hotter weather, although the humidity has little effect. The ball temperature also has quite a considerable effect so ideally keep your golf balls warm overnight before playing in colder weather. Do not attempt to boil them or put them in the oven, though as they might explode!

To choose the best ball for you it is necessary to decide whether you are a high-spin (fast) swinger, or a low-spin (slower) hitter. In an ideal world, but depending on the launch angle of the ball, a high-spin (fast) player will be better off using wound, low-spin balls (surlyn), though by their nature they are less controllable than balata. Avoid solid golf balls. Tour players hit the balata ball with an initial velocity of about 155mph, and a spin rate of around 4100 rpm. A wound surlyn ball spins at about 3700rpm as it leaves the

clubface; a two-piece ball about 3100rpm. Every five mph increase adds eight yards to the distance. John Daly hits the ball with an intiial velocity of around 180mph! By contrast the average club golfer is in the 100-130mph range. This is the initial ball velocity - not the speed of the clubhead as it strikes the ball.

The launch angle is critical, with an angle of between 14 and 18 degrees being the best with the driver.

Balata balls give better control but less distance; surlyn balls give more distance but less control. There are balls on the market now that claim to do both and a wound ball might satisfy both camps.

Golf ball technologys does, as you can see, make quite a big difference. I would recommend that you find a ball that works for you and stick with it, rather than changing too often.

3 The Swing

THE WHOLE POINT of getting the grip, stance and aim correct is to get you into a position to swing the club. The problem is that most people get too involved in the club rather than in turning the body back and through.

Just as many beginners to golf become overly concerned with the ball, so many more experienced golfers concentrate too much on the club.

The swing is a two-lever movement and I will build it here in little parts. Then we'll put it all together, for it is really just one flowing movement.

THE BACKSWING

I'll begin with the backswing: from a good address position the *lower back* turns to the right. That pulls the shoulders round; they move the arms; the arms move the club. *The shoulders must never instigate the backswing.*

Weight Transfer

As you turn, your weight transfers towards the right side. Here is a similar situation: if you want to throw a tennis ball as far as you can what do you do? First you lean your upper body backwards, moving the weight onto your back foot to get a coiling action, then your throwing arm moves back; then your body weight is thrown forwards and finally your arm moves forwards, releasing the ball and extending on after it. Note carefully the sequence: weight back; arm back; weight forwards; arm forwards. It's the same in golf, except the hand holds the club, not the ball.

The weight transfer to the back foot is essential to wind up the power you need to throw the club through impact. Try this: stand with your feet together and your legs absolutely straight. Without moving your legs at all, throw the tennis ball. It won't go as far as it would if you had thrown it as I described a few moments ago. This simple experiment should show you how important the legs are in golf; without good legwork you will never achieve your full potential. You must also recognize that the legs are only a platform on which your body is balanced; they don't work on their own.

Cocking the Wrists

At waist height the hands should still be holding the club level to the line of the shoulders, not behind them. From there the wrists cock, lifting the club higher and creating the second lever in the swing. The left arm stays as extended as possible, not rigidly straight but firm. This adds extra width to the swing. The wrists also cock at this point, lifting the club higher. Some good players begin the wrist cock a little earlier than this, so that by the time their hands have reached waist height going back the club is almost vertical. As long as the left arm is well extended and the hands have not moved behind the

body line, this is perfectly satisfactory.

As the backswing progresses the weight continues to transfer to the right. Many higher handicap players sway or reverse pivot at

Ensure you do not move the club behind you too early.

this stage but the good golfer ensures that his weight is finely balanced above the right knee, that knee taking the strain. If, at the top of the backswing, you can feel that your right knee is where your weight is balanced you are doing fine.

The head should try to stay fairly quiet through the backswing but it does slide slightly right. Many good players slightly turn the head away in the backswing.

The shoulders have, by this stage, continued to turn as far back as they can go, to at least ninety degrees to the target line: in effect you now have your back facing directly at the target.

Common Faults

The majority of players never turn far enough in the backswing. Work on moving your shoulders a little further round: you will find quite a big difference in your power. You should be in the position where, at the top of your backswing, the left shoulder is **behind** the ball. This proves that you have turned far enough and that your weight has moved correctly onto the right side. If your left shoulder is ahead of the ball you have probably created a reverse pivot which will throw you off balance as you swing through. One major fault in the swing is to tilt the shoulders: they should turn, not tilt too much. Take a careful look at yours.

The Arm Position

The left arm should have maintained its extension and the right elbow folded to a 90 degree angle to the plane of the swing, which is itself at 90 degrees to the spine at address (as well as impact). The wrists are here fully cocked and ideally the left wrist will be flat, rather than cupped or bowed. Some players cannot achieve this, but do try to avoid a cupped wrist, as that will lead to problems in the downswing.

One major fault among higher handicappers, and which can sometimes afflict better players too, is that of the flying right elbow. At the very top of the backswing your right elbow should be tucked in and pointing straight down at your right heel. If it points too far behind you, you are in an incorrect position.

Left: A common problem – by failing to turn the shoulders enough they tend to tilt rather than turn, resulting in a lower hand position at the top, a possible cause of a hook.

Right: The correct position.

The Swing Plane

A word here about the swing plane and upright or flat swings. Taller players tend to swing more upright than shorter players. You should try to swing on plane whilst still maintaining your balance. Most poor players swing too flat, bringing the club inside the line too early in the moveaway and not getting enough height at the top of the backswing. Halfway into the backswing the shaft of the club should be parallel to its position at address, the butt end pointing directly at the ball.

By getting height into the swing you increase the swing arc and thus the speed of the club-head. That means extra distance.

If your swing tends towards the flat side, try this little experiment. In front of a mirror, go to the top of your backswing as normal: can you see your hands clear above your head? If not, push your hands a little higher and watch carefully the extra extension this gives you in the left arm. The hands should be clearly visible above the head – that's the position you want. Work on it until it becomes natural. You won't lose control of the club, although at first it will seem strange, as all changes do.

The Downswing

What starts the downswing? Many used to suggest that the shoulders were instrumental in starting the downswing, though this theory has now been supplanted by a general consensus that it is the left foot which kicks the downswing into life.

The Weight Transfer

At the top of the backswing the left foot has to rolled to its instep, though I never recommend letting the heel rise. As with the example of throwing the tennis ball I gave earlier, the left, forward foot has to go down flat to help transfer the weight to the left side. If you tried to throw the ball with your left foot off the ground you'd get no real power, so the left foot must go down flat again, pushed by the left knee. That pulls the weight across to the left side. At the same time your shoulders begin turning to the left, pulling the arms round with them. The left shoulder lifts as it begins to turn, pushing the right shoulder down. That pushes the club down on the inside path, the back edge of the cone. Think carefully about this and fully understand it.

At this stage the clubhead stays high because the wrists must not uncock yet. If they uncock too early you will lose all your power. You should almost feel that you even slightly cock them a touch more as you begin the down-swing, really letting the clubhead trail behind.

The right arm swings down inside the line, to attack the ball from slightly inside. You should have the feeling that your right elbow is more tucked into the body, attacking the ball from slightly inside the target line. If the club comes down too far to the front you will have been casting the club, risking a slice.

By having an imaginary target just ahead of, and outside the ball, you will get a better impression of the way to attack the ball from the inside.

The aim becomes to hit the ball, then to hit this imaginary target as you sweep the clubhead through.

By waist height coming down,

Note how, as the downswing begins, the right elbow drops – look again at the picture on page 23 (right) to see the previous position.

25

the club shaft should still be vertical, showing that the wrists have not yet uncocked. By this stage the weight is transferring to the left, not as a sway, but rather as a turn, the hips clearing out of the way to allow space for the arms to swing the club through impact. Contrary to what some people think, it is not the wrists and hands that accelerate the club-head through impact, but the shoulders turning out of the way. Power comes from the big muscles in the body, the legs, hips and shoulders: if they turn properly they pull the hands down, which in turn pull the clubhead.

Impact

The impact position is *not* a replica of the address position. At impact the hips have already half turned to the left and have moved slightly later-ally to the left. The head remains slightly behind the ball.

Good timing is essential in the golf swing. If you turn out of the way too early you will block the

Before impact the hands have reached their address position as the wrists uncock as late as possible to produce power.

26

shot; turn too late and you might hook it as you try to work your hands too much through impact to catch up. By impact you should have turned your hips out of the way and your hands will have reached their address position with the left arm forming a straight line down through the club shaft, although, as at address, your hands will probably be slightly ahead of the ball.

The Wrists and Hands

To get to this position the wrists will have had to uncock. Halfway down they were still cocked but from there they work overtime, really pulling the club through the impact zone as fast as possible to create power. The left wrist is again flat, as it was at address and at the top of the backswing. This guarantees that you will square the clubhead at impact, to hit a straight shot, providing you are aiming straight.

You should have the feeling that you are putting pressure on the clubface, rather as though you were banging it against a block of wood, or an old tyre as Henry Cotton used to teach, though that might damage your wrist. If you want to feel the power at impact,

hit through long grass: to get the clubhead through you have to drag it through correctly. That, in fact, is a very good exercise. Another very good exercise is to swing the club back only to the point where your arms are horizontal, but cock the wrists fully: then swing through to a mirror image, the hands stopping at waist height. In the interim the idea is to get as much clubhead speed as you can, making a swishing sound with the clubhead. A further very good exercise is, with an 8-iron, to hit golf balls with your feet together, not moving your legs at all during the swing; that really makes you use your hands in the golf swing.

Post Impact

Post impact is quite important, not for what you can do to the ball – nothing, because it's already fifteen feet away by the time you realize you've hit it – but because it proves that what you have done before is correct. The body should continue to turn, proving that you have still been accelerating at impact to produce maximum power, and the hands release, or turn the club, the right hand rotating round the left. Many people get totally hung up on release, but it is not really something you should worry about as it will happen quite naturally providing you are in the right position at impact.

If you want to experience what the perfect release feels like, try swinging a towel firmly rolled up, imagining you are really hitting a golf ball with it. Your hands have to work hard to re-lease the power at 'impact' and you will build up a very good under-standing in your muscles as to how a correct release should feel.

Left: *Just after impact the club is still being thrown towards the target.*

Opposite right: *From a different angle the hands can clearly be seen to have released, yet the head has stayed down. Only from now will it lift towards the target.*

Steering the Club

Some players try to steer the club after impact, although there are some professionals who say this is bad. In fact, if you do try to steer the club straight towards the target you have probably swung it correctly because you are swinging too fast to change direction. The clubhead has its own momentum. If you have pulled the clubhead inside the line too quickly after impact you will probably have hit a hook. If you feel you want to steer it, then do

so. We do it on our short shots and our putts, so why not on full shots?

The Finish

Old pictures of Seve at full tilt used to show him leaning back after impact in what was known as the 'reverse C position', the club virtually wrapped round his neck. This position is probably what has caused his bad back. A good finishing position is one in which you are balanced and facing the target; the club has travelled straight through impact and has finished its arc, and ideally your left knee will be fairly straight.

Whatever you look like at the finish there is, really, only one way to tell if you've hit a good shot. Look where the ball finishes! That's the only thing that matters.

Above: The club follows its arc perfectly, being here in almost a mirror image of the backswing. Don't swing the club inside too quickly going through – steer the ball.

Opposite: The finish, the body turned to face the target and perfectly balanced and upright, the club having been thrown through completely.

4 Tee-shots

'DRIVE FOR SHOW; putt for dough' is an old saying in golf, yet like so many old wives' tales it is little more than a myth. Ben Hogan once said that driving was the most important part of golf, and he wasn't far wrong, because unless you can drive for show you will never be in a position to putt for dough.

The tee shot is, I believe, the most important in golf; don't let anyone tell you different. The driver is a very individual club, just like the putter, so take care when selecting one. Don't just buy the one that comes with the set of clubs. A golf professional will help you to select a driver that matches your swing speed and temperament. Different shafts and different sized heads will all affect the type of shots you will hit.

Many players have drivers that are slightly turned in, the face slightly closed to counter the effect of a slice, the driving fault of most higher handicappers. Personally I don't like them, preferring to see the face sit square to the ball at address, but it's up to each player to choose what suits him.

Metal-headed drivers are more popular these days, partly because they have a lower centre of gravity and thus hit the ball higher. Graphite shafts are also more popular as, being lighter, they allow the manufacturer to put more weight in the head, which helps to increase the speed at impact. You can also use a metal-headed driver off the fairway without too much difficulty.

Although most people will automatically think of the driver when you mention tee-shots, you can use almost any club; it depends on the shot you have. A long, straight hole may well demand the driver; but we shall also look at tee-shots on short par-3 holes. If anything, that shot is more important than the drive on a 500-yard (460 metre) par-5. Some holes demand a lay-up, possibly with a 3- or a 5-wood or maybe a long iron. Yet all tee-shots have much in common, apart from the fact that you can place the ball in the most perfect position imaginable, within reason.

The tee-box extends two club-lengths back from the markers, a fact that is used by professionals when choosing which club to use, particularly on short holes. Possibly more important than how far back you tee the ball is the side on which you tee it. Normally, it is best to tee on the same side as any hazards, to play away from the trouble. Beware of any overhanging branches between ball and target and also of the type of shot you normally hit (fade or draw) and of any wind, particularly if the teeing area or the green is protected from wind by trees.

Look at the tops of the trees between you and the target, and also at clouds; they never lie about which way the wind is blowing.

How high you tee the ball depends on your normal game and the club you are using, as well as on the hole itself. Most players tee the ball too low, especially when using the driver. The average driver has a loft of between ten and twelve degrees, though the metal-headed drivers have a lower centre of gravity and thus hit the ball higher. If you watch top professionals off the tee they hit the ball really high (and hard). Although you don't want to sky it you should be looking to get it a bit higher, except into a strong wind. Technically it has been found that a ball will fly furthest when hit at an initial trajectory of eighteen degrees. With a twelve degree driver this would suggest that you should hit the ball with the clubface rising at six degrees, which is something to work on!

Ironically, by teeing it too low you actually risk hitting it too high because with the ball low, you are subconsciously aware that you need to get down to the ball. To do this you tend to come down more steeply into the back of the ball and, as you know, a descending blow means the ball goes up – golf is a game of opposites.

Understanding Driving Technique

The best drives are hit with the club-head coming in low and on line, taking the ball just after the nadir of the swing. A shot off grass with an iron takes the ball just before the nadir of the swing.

The vital point about driving is that the clubhead must spend as long as possible close to the ground. In technical terms this means having a wider swing arc. The long, low swing arc is ideal for the driver, particularly if you can accelerate the clubhead through impact.

For extra distance some players stand a fraction closed at address, thus extending the backswing by allowing more shoulder turn. However, that can cause problems in clearing the hips sufficiently quickly to allow the arms to swing the club through, so be very careful . Standing very slightly open to the ball for a drive can help you get the arms through better though it slightly shortens the backswing.

Finding the best thing for you will take some time and practice; all I can do is to help you understand the various techniques used by different good golfers.

With a full shot of any type it is vital that the shoulders are fully turned. More people fail to hit their drives to their full potential because of a failure to turn their shoulders than for any other reason.

Extending the Backswing

To get the best out of your drives you need to have the clubhead, at impact, travelling as fast as you can, without losing control. To do this you need a wide and fast down-swing. Extending the backswing is relatively simple if you will only try it. At the practice or driving range just hit half-a-dozen shots as you normally do; then try to hit half-a-dozen by extending the backswing a little more, stretching it back and up as far as you can without losing control. At first it might appear that you feel you have lost control over the clubhead at the top of the back-

swing, but the chances are that you won't have.

What you should feel – because it happens – is that your left arm has remained straighter through the backswing and this in itself extends the length of the backswing by pushing the club on a wider arc. You should also feel that you are swinging more upright and you probably will be. That is not a bad thing and will lead to a straighter shot, particularly if you normally draw the ball.

You can, as I said, also extend the apparent shoulder turn by standing very slightly closed, though do be careful to aim the clubface perfectly as well as having the ball far enough forward. Standing closed does mean that you may risk hooking the ball if you don't catch it properly, so be very careful about this. Try it on the practice range first.

Hitting the Ball Harder

The other way to hit the ball further is to hit it harder. However, altering your swing speed for one particular shot is not something I would recommend: if you want to swing faster, you must do it all the time.

This is something to begin changing on the practice range. Get

Stand very slightly open for a drive with the ball opposite the left heel. Never tee it too high.

To get maximum power the shoulders must really turn on the backswing; get the left shoulder well behind the ball.

into the rhythm of your normal swing and then try to increase the speed gradually, but without losing control. Of course you will lose control some of the time as you build up the speed, but once the increased speed becomes your standard you will retain control. A word of warning here: don't get too ambitious. Control your swing even if you can't quite achieve the speed you want. Control and rhythm are more important than mere speed.

Yet no amount of speed will do any good unless you catch the ball square when the clubhead is travelling at its fastest. Quitting on shots is something that higher handicappers do; don't let it happen to you.

Better players are often referred to as 'hands players' because they use their hands – or more correctly their wrists – through the shot. The use of the hands, or wrists, starts at the beginning of the backswing. As a better-than-average player you already know that the downswing, or more correctly forward swing, begins whilst the club is still being swung back. The exact moment when the weight begins to transfer to the left varies slightly with each player according to his balance, but before the club has reached the top of its backswing the lower body will start the forward swing by throwing the weight towards the left side.

The Perfect Swing

A perfect swing will have the head fairly steady above the centre of gravity in the backswing, with the proviso that the centre of gravity moves slightly right; then in the through swing the lower body begins turning left first. It must not sway, but turn, with the aim of getting the body facing the target just after impact.

As the downswing starts the hips begin to turn but it is the arms that need some attention if you are to be a seriously good player. Try to keep the left arm reasonably straight, widening the swing arc, as you begin the forward swing. Keep the swing plane on the inside, which is often misinterpreted as tucking the right elbow in to the right side of the body: the swing must flow and by tucking the right elbow in too much you will take the natural rhythm out of your swing.

From the top of the backswing just ensure that the plane of the downswing is from inside the line. No doubt you have, at some time in your golf career, 'cast' the club from the top, throwing it outside the line in an effort to get more power. With experience comes more control and the shot from in-to-on-line-to-in is the correct one.

It can help to have a mini target

just outside the ball to aim at. Instead of looking at the ball have in mind a blade of grass just in front of and outside the ball. Your aim is to hit the ball and then hit this mini target. See the illustration below. By doing this you will automatically bring the club down from inside the line and strike the ball well, with a hint of draw.

I mentioned the role of the wrists. The feeling from the top is that the shoulders are moving first, rather than the arms. As the left shoulder begins turning and lifting, the right shoulder drops. The arms remain fairly straight as the hands drop but the clubhead lags behind in the downswing. A really good player will have his hands almost above the ball whilst the clubhead is still waist high. From there the wrists really unleash the power and accelerate the clubhead through impact with a massive amount of leverage, producing a very hard shot. It is, as you can see, the unhinging of the wrists that produces this late power.

This does take some practice and it is essential to have the correct shaft flex. Too stiff a shaft would stop you returning the clubface to square.

Imagine a mini-target in front of and just outside the ball. The low tee is the ball-target line; the high tee is the mini-target. By trying to hit that after you hit the ball your swing will continue slightly in-to-out and you will put a nice draw on the ball.

With any full shot a full follow-through is essential; with the driver this is even more important. Make sure you finish well balanced and turn completely through the shot.

Short Tee-Shots

Not all tee-shots need to be hit as far as possible. Some demand extra accuracy and some demand a lay-up. Before you play any shot you should have in mind where you want the ball to be for your next shot, as in a game of chess. On a hole which dog-legs you need to decide whether you want to cut the corner as close as possible, or to play to the outside of the dog-leg, lengthening the second shot but probably giving you a better view of the green. Golf architects are clever.

Using a 3-wood or 1-iron off the tee can be effective when you need accuracy above all and the distance you lose against the driver is probably less than you might imagine. I often think most players would be better off using a 3-wood on the first tee, as the number of mis-hit drives on that hole is generally enormous.

When laying up, make sure you know the exact distance to the hazard or until you run out of fairway. Give yourself at least a 10 per cent margin of error and take into account the wind, any slope and also the firmness of the fairway, as a

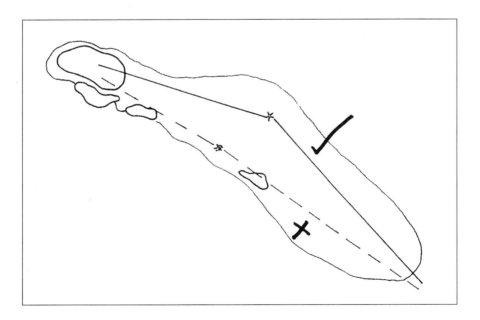

Think before you hit! Choose the ideal place from which to hit your next shot.

ball will bounce and roll more on a firm, tight lie than in wet or lush grass.

Par-3 Tee Shots

Par-3 tee-shots are possibly the most important, for you have only one opportunity to get the ball on the green and, hopefully, fairly close to the pin. Most professionals use a tee-peg to set the ball up, pushing the peg into the ground so that just the top is showing. One problem many non-professionals have with this shot is that they try to take the ball off the tee-peg as

On a very short par-3, particularly to a green below the tee, I would sit the ball well up and clip it from underneath, hitting it almost straight up in the air. Correct club selection is vital.

cleanly as they would with the driver. All this does is to lose distance and probably direction.

The idea is to hit down into the back of the ball just as with any other iron shot. You still need a divot. Always have in mind that you should want to 'kill' the tee-peg, taking a reasonable divot at the same time. If you are not taking a divot off a tee-peg on par-3s with a medium or short iron you are not hitting down enough. Play the ball slightly further back in your stance, or better, spend a few weeks playing the ball off the turf. That will make you go down to it more.

On a very short par-3 (less than about 140 yards/130 metres), you are obviously using a well-lofted club and the tendency is to clip the ball up from underneath. If you do this, make sure you have enough club to hit the back of the green because, when the ball flies higher, it flies shorter.

One exception might be a very short par-3, particularly to a green well below the level of the tee. Here you need a high shot that will come down almost vertically by the flag, with no run. In these circumstances I might be tempted to tee the ball fairly high and hit a well-lofted club (wedge or 9-iron) under the ball, getting it airborne very steeply. You must know your distances with this

shot as it is not as easy as it looks.

I once used a similar shot at the infamous 17th at Sawgrass, a shot across an alligator-infested lake to a fairly small green. Here again the distance suggested a 7-iron but by teeing the ball higher and using a 6-iron, the ball flew higher and landed steeper than it would otherwise have done. I got a two.

Most par-3 greens have their trouble near the front so it is always a good idea to be absolutely certain that you have the correct club. If in doubt, and with no real trouble going long, take one more club than you think. If the front is clear and there is trouble long, err on the short side, leaving you a little run up or chip. Stay away from trouble.

Driving in Strong Wind

Finally, driving in strong wind can cause problems, but only if you let the wind get the better of you. Most problems are caused by trying to hit the ball too hard into the wind and

Opposite:In strong wind stay more relaxed and balanced and hit smoother, not harder. Make a full swing but try to keep your balance better; that will result in a smoother strike. Hold the follow-through to no more than shoulder height. Tee the ball fairly low.

what happens is that the player tries to get through the ball faster and ends up swaying.

In strong wind take more time to get yourself settled. Tee the ball as normal, no higher, no lower. Wait for the wind to die down a little if it is gusting. Swing even more smoothly than normal and stand slightly closed to lengthen the backswing. You may need your feet slightly wider apart than normal as this helps you balance better and very slightly lowers your centre of gravity. You must swing smoothly, really trying to stay as still as possible. Don't fight the wind because you won't win!

Let the wind help you. If it is from the left, play into it first to allow the ball to come round, but don't try to draw it as that will end up as a hook. If the wind is from the right, hit out to the right first and let the ball come round to the left.

Much has been written about hitting directly into the wind. The best thing to do is to keep the ball fairly low, as this increases the top-spin and keeps it going longer. To keep the ball low either play it slightly further back in your stance and, once again, stand slightly closed, or stand square and have the ball further forwards, the club-face connecting higher up the ball and almost topping it. The follow-through is cut off, the hands finishing no higher than about shoulder height, the club not finishing round the back as normal on a full shot. By holding the follow-through you should also be able to steer the ball a little better.

Practising in wind is the only way you will learn to play these shots effectively, but don't practise long shots in wind for more than about thirty minutes as it will adversely affect your balance.

5 The Long Game

FAIRWAY WOODS

ALTHOUGH not the only ones the most popular fairway woods are the 3-wood and the 5-wood. In the United States the 7-wood is also very popular, particularly for senior and lady golfers.

The 3-wood

The 3-wood is an ideal club to use on many tees, particularly if you need to lay the ball up to avoid running out of fairway. It's also ideal off the tee downwind as it hits the ball higher than a driver, so catching more tail-wind. Off the fairway, though, you need to have a very good lie to hit the 3-wood. In semi-rough it's fine, but only if the ball is sitting up. The aim is to get distance with this club, rather than pinpoint accuracy so if you are faced with a small target consider another option. It is normally used for shots in the region of about 200–230 yards (180–200 metres).

With the 3-wood the aim is to sweep the ball off the fairway, with no divot. Like the driver the best swing arc for this club will bring the clubhead into the impact zone low and straight. It does not hit the ball on the upswing, as does the driver off a tee-peg, but hits it straight forwards. The loft on the face will get the ball airborne.

A really good practice routine with the 3-wood, which will help you fully understand the shot, is to place two tees in the ground, one where the ball would be, the second about 5in (12cm) further forwards, towards the target. Then swing the club to take both tee-pegs out of the ground. Most higher handicappers try to hit the ball up; better players hit it forwards.

The 5-wood

This is possibly the friendliest club in the bag and can be used to manufacture shots in the region of anything from about 170 to 220 yards (155–180 metres). It can be used off a tee on a par-3, despite the macho idea of always using an iron; use what you need, not what your opponent uses. Off the tee, play it low but don't hit down on it. Hit through, sweeping the ball away, just as with the 3-wood. The loft on the face will get the ball airborne . Although it has the same loft as a 4-iron, it will normally go higher than the iron and travel a little further, so if you have a difficult 4-iron shot (perhaps to carry a hazard), think of using the 5-wood. The extra height it hits the ball will bring it down more softly, so it's ideal for small greens. Out of the rough grass the 5-wood will normally give you good distance, the flat sole of the club parting the grass and getting to the ball straighter than an iron. Be sensible, though, and don't use it in thick, clingy rough and don't hit down with this club in the rough: it is made to slide through the grass and hit the ball face-on.

Its other prime use is in manufacturing shots, particularly high fades round and over trees, for example. By having the ball slightly more forwards in your stance and standing open you can play perfect high fades, the ball coming down softly.

It really is the most versatile club in the bag so don't leave it at home!

Above: *A smooth finish is necessary. Never try to overhit the ball.*

Opposite: *A 5-wood off the fairway is an ideal club. Have the ball central and sweep through it, rather than hitting down into the back of it. Swing smoothly.*

To hit the ball higher have it slightly forward in the stance and again swing smoothly.
Extend the club through towards the target.

THE LONG IRONS

You should be looking for distance from the long irons (2, 3 and 4) rather than pinpoint accuracy so if you have a really tight target where a wayward shot will be punished, think again, possibly laying up and giving yourself an easy chip or pitch. Don't waste shots. The ball will fly fairly low with the long irons and will run on landing (unless the grass is very wet or lush), so don't just think about where the ball will land but where it will run to.

Never rush the swing; let the club do the work. Trying to force extra distance out of a club just will not work. The take-away should be smooth and low and you might find it helpful to hover the club behind the ball at address, rather than grounding it. That will make for a smooth-er, lower moveaway as there is no necessity to pick the club up. The same applies, incidentally, to the driver and other woods.

I'll emphasize again that you do not want to hit the ball up, you want to hit it forwards. The loft on the clubface will do that so your swing

At address the ball should be central in your stance, the hands slightly ahead.

should be low and long, taking only a very shallow divot, though a fairly long one. Ensure you get a full shoulder turn and really drive your right leg through the shot, really pushing the body round to the left. Use your big muscles. The ideal shot with the long irons is a slight draw so attack the ball from the inside, again using the idea of a second 'ball' just ahead of and slightly outside the real one.

A positive swing will result in a good finish, the body not leaning to one side. Many golfers finish their shot with a long iron leaning slightly to the right, normally a sign that the ball has gone that way too. You must be as balanced at the finish as you were at address.

Before we finish this chapter a word about using the driver from the fairway. Most metal-headed drivers can safely be used off a good lie and will hit the

A low, slow takeaway is essential with the long irons.

ball long and low, with a slight fade. If you have a long shot that you want to slide to the right round some trees, consider the driver, playing it very slightly forward with a slightly open stance. Avoid swinging it too flat as that will just hook it left.

Extend through the shot, keeping your head down and steering the club at the target.

The long irons and fairway woods should figure regularly in your practice routines as learning how to manoeuvre the ball with them will greatly strengthen your repertoire of shots. Once you have warmed up the swing with the short irons, move on to the long irons and try to hit a fade, a draw, a high shot and a low shot in succession. By altering the position of the ball and your stance these shots become easy and you will have the ability to produce them. If you can add them to your repertoire in practice, they will be there when you need them on the golf course.

6 Approach Shots

WHAT IS an approach shot? Any shot which is aimed at the green, with the intention of hitting it is, technically, an approach shot. Here, though, I am leaving out chipping, pitching and bunker shots, which will be included in a later chapter, and I have already dealt with long irons and fairway woods which can be hit at the green. Basically that leaves any shot with the medium and short irons, from the 5-iron to the 9-iron. You can use the wedge and the lob-wedge but I have really dealt with those in the short game chapter as they are rather specialized. The medium and short irons are very easy to use. Unlike the long irons distance is not the only vital requirement: accuracy is.

The 5- and 6-irons

To begin, let's take the 5- or 6-iron, which you will normally be using when you have between about 170 and 140 yards (155–130 metres) to go. A normal approach shot with either of these is not too difficult.

When deciding which club to use, look carefully at the distance, taking into account not only the distance to the centre of the green, if there are any markers to help you on the course, but the contour of the land, the wind and the size of the green. The chances are that, from this distance, you won't be able to tell whether the flag is central, or to the front or back; however, you will be able to see whether it is left, right or centre of the green, so you know which side you should be aiming at. A normal shot with these clubs will hit the ball fairly high and bring it down with only a small amount of roll, depending on the receptiveness of the green.

The normal shot will have the ball central in the stance, your body aimed parallel to the target, and you will take a full swing. If you tend to slightly cut these shots you need to be aiming at the left side of the green to allow the ball to come round. If you draw the ball aim to the right side of the green but not outside it. Accuracy is vital.

Opposite: With the medium irons (here shown on the tee – it was a nicer picture!) you need the ball central at address (top), the left arm and club forming a straight line. The takeaway (bottom) stays wide and in front of the body.

Opposite, top: *The sequence continue with the top of the backswing complete, the hands above the head, the left shoulder behind the ball.*

Opposite, bottom: *The downswing is kicked into action, the right shoulder dropping the club down inside the line. Note how the hands have dropped but the wrist-cock remains, leaving the clubhead behind.*

Above: *The hands continue dropping but the wrists remain cocked. A last-minute uncocking releases the power.*

Top: *Just after impact the hands continue throwing the club towards the target, but look how the head has remained still.*

Bottom: *The body turns completely, facing the target and still throwing the club up and forward.*

The Higher Shot

With a small green to aim at, your best shot will probably be a higher – and thus slightly shorter – shot. To play this, have the ball a little further forwards in your stance and stand a little more open. You are going to put slice spin on the ball, so aim to the left side of the green. The body turn should begin from the lower back, as always, and a really full turn is essential, the hands taken back fairly high (though don't pick the club up). A full acceleration through the ball is essential, really dragging the club down into the back of the ball. A lot of hand movement is important in this shot, the follow-through being high and on line, the arms being extended towards the target before finishing well round your back.

The ball will fly high but a little shorter, landing very softly, so make sure you have enough club. If the distance to the pin suggests a 7-iron but you want to hit high to a small green, take the 6-iron. There's no problem going past the pin; in most cases, because not so many golfers go past the pin, you will find the back of the green is softer and more receptive.

The Lower Shot

On other occasions you will want to hit the ball in fairly low, perhaps because you have overhanging branches in the way. Here take an extra club or possibly even two clubs more, play the ball back in your stance and hood the face a slightly. Take a three-quarter backswing, hit down sharply and hold the follow-through, not letting the hands release. The ball will get airborne and will run on once it lands.

Much of this is common-sense but golfers often forget things on the course. When you're practising, work on these unusual shots because once you master them they are no longer unusual!

The 7- and 8-irons

The 7- and 8-irons are used in the region of 140–120 yards (130–110 metres) and are clubs for 100 per cent accuracy, so never try to overhit them. If you think the shot is a strong 8-iron, change clubs and make it an easy 7-iron. You get no points for hitting the longest 8-iron in your group!

Technique

The shoulder turn must be full, though with some shots you will only be swinging about three-quarters. The same technique as we used for the 5- and 6-irons applies if you want to hit the ball higher, but otherwise have it central in your stance, so that the clubface catches it on the way down. You must hit down with these clubs. I would normally recommend that you stand a couple of inches open to the target to get the hips well out of the way early, but make sure your shoulders are parallel to the target line.

With the short clubs, the amount of fade or draw you can achieve will be less than on longer shots, so I would always suggest that you aim directly at the flag, unless you are deliberately aiming at the fat of the green for safety. Don't try to work the ball too much with these irons, unless playing in a very strong wind, when you must be aware of what the wind will do.

A full shoulder turn is necessary; never half hit an approach.

Left: Hit through the shot but keep your head down and your body turning – don't sway.

Below: A full follow-through proves you have hit the shot correctly.

7 Difficult Shots

TREES

TREES ARE lovely to look at but a pain when they get between the ball and the green! Always carefully consider what type of shot you need to get past them, either going round, under or over them.

If you want to go over, make sure you can safely get the ball high enough but keep in mind that by hitting it higher you will hit less distance, so you will need one or more clubs extra. Play the ball a little further forwards in an open stance, swing the club more steeply (don't confuse that with picking the club up) and release your hands through impact, following through to a very high finish. If you get to the stage where you need a 5-iron or more, the club to use is the 5-wood which will get the ball high.

Keeping the ball low is easy. Take more club than you normally need for the distance, play the ball back in a square stance, hood the

With a high shot make sure you have enough loft on the clubface and play the ball forward in an open stance.

clubface, swing back about three-quarters and hold the follow-through, your hands finishing no higher than about chest height going through.

Drawing and fading the ball round trees is easy and you obviously have the ability to play these shots. The important thing about playing from near trees is that you know exactly what shot will work before you play it; never just hope it will work. If in doubt, use another option.

The Rough

We all visit the rough and any visit to a golf tournament will show you just how often professionals hit their drives into the rough. However, the difference between them and the average club golfer is that the professionals normally still escape with a par. Why? Basically because they use their common sense. No professional would even consider some of the shots that you see amateur golfers trying to play from the rough. In really deep rough the only aim is to get the ball back on the fairway: it's that simple. This is no time for heroics: the only option is to find a suitable place on the short grass from where you can play your next shot and, using a well lofted club, knock the ball out to that target.

A sand-wedge is good in heavy rough and the shot is virtually the same as in a bunker, the aim being to get the club under the ball, hitting down hard behind it, dislodging as much grass as you can along with the ball. The swing is fairly upright and steep with a real downward acceleration and as full a follow-through as you can manage. Be aware that in heavy rough the grass tends to snag the clubhead, pulling it round towards the left. You may need to aim further right to compensate for this.

In light rough you will find it easier to achieve distance though be careful if the ball is sitting up, as many players then try to hit down under the ball and end up scooping it, with a loss of distance. The ball should be swept off the surface just as from a fairway bunker. This might mean gripping down the club a little whilst standing normally, the clubhead being further off the ground, but don't hit down too much.

I suggested earlier that the 5-wood is a perfect club for these shots. It really does the job. Again, play sensibly, never attempting a shot you only think you can play: know you can play it!

Left: *In rough play the ball back in your stance and use a well lofted club.*

Below: *Only take a three-quarter swing to ensure you do not move your lower body. Stay balanced.*

Below: *Get right down to the ball, digging under it and not leaving anything to chance.*

Right: *Continue through the shot as hard as you can.*

Slopes

Shots off slopes can be difficult to judge because the ball will follow the contour of the slope. On a slope with the ball below your feet flex the knees a little more than normal, aim slightly left (up the slope) and play the ball back in your stance. Only take a three-quarter swing or you will lose your balance.

The opposite is true with the ball above your feet. You should be standing almost upright and gripping down the club as far as is necessary. It's not a good idea to use a long club (no more than a 6-iron) on severe slopes or you will risk hitting the ball fat. The swing will be flatter to enable you to catch the ball and this does cause a draw so you need to compensate by aiming right and having the ball forward in your stance.

From a downhill shot the ball will always fade, so stand open to

For a downhill shot let the club follow the contours, not coming down too steeply. Sweep the ball downhill. It will fade.

the target and aim a little left. The ball might not fly very high so beware of any hazards you have to carry to the green. A low-flying shot will not stop very well on the green,

so it might be sensible to lay up.

Uphill shots tend to be harder but there is one important point. Apart from standing slightly closed, aiming right and swinging a little flatter, on an uphill shot you really need to work the lower body through the shot, the right knee really kicking round hard into the impact zone, driving the bodyweight uphill. It's not sufficient to allow the left leg to pull the weight round; the right side must drive, pushing the bodyweight across.

On a downhill shot you need less club than normal and the reverse is true going uphill.

Going uphill really kick your right leg round, pushing your body weight up the slope.

8 The Short Game

WITHOUT DOUBT the short game is the most important part of golf. Even in top tournaments, you will see players missing the green with almost alarming regularity, yet most of them still escape with a par.

All professionals agree that the ability to chip and pitch to within a few inches of the pin is the most highly regarded skill in golf as well as being the one which brings most benefits. For the average-to-good player, honing the skills of pitching and chipping is vital, particularly on long par-4s where it might not be possible to reach the green in regulation. The same is true of par-3s where you could almost take bets on the tee about all four players in a fourball hitting the green. On charity and company golf days that's a sure way of raising funds for needy causes. Even on shorter par-5s where a good player might get close in two, the ability to play the third shot to within birdie putt range is an ideal way of gaining strokes against par.

Choosing the right shot is vital and in this section we shall look at certain situations and how best to play them. One point to ponder is that for the better player there is no single way to play any shot. Using your imagination to conjure up the right shot is vital, but it only comes with practice and experience. One very good way to gain that experience is, when you practise, to replicate the type of situations you encountered during your last round of golf, particularly any which gave you problems. Try several different ways of playing the shot, using different clubs until you find the one which suits you and the situation the best. Keep on doing this to continually expand your repertoire of shots.

Historically golf used to be played along the ground. That is not to say that the ball never got airborne, but that the mainly links courses were designed with a clear run-up area to the green with no bunkers in front of it. Accuracy in running the ball in low was paramount and particularly important in the windy conditions normally prevailing on the coast. At that time greens were not watered, so any shot coming in high would just have bounced on over the back of the green.

As golf grew in importance in the United States, the trend changed from the flat links courses with this run-up area, to the type of greens we find today. Greens needed watering in the hot summers of the southern United States so they had to be elevated to help them drain better after the twice-daily soaking. That obviously made them more receptive and 'target golf' came into its own.

The days of the 6-iron run-up shot from 140 yards (130 metres) are probably gone forever, though those who do play on true links courses still have the opportunity to play this type of shot. Certainly it tests your accuracy in both distance and direction and is a good teaching exercise, but in truth it has only limited use on the golf course, though could be used when you are under some overhanging trees and need to hit the ball a good distance yet still keep it low.

However, anyone who can accurately run the ball in from 100 yards (90 metres) or more should have no problems in coping with a thirty-yard chip-and-run, so the exercise does have its benefits.

Chip versus Pitch

Knowing when to play a particular shot is vital and the better player will always have at least a couple of options when facing any situation. It all comes down to your ability to play each shot (probably reflecting what you have practised most). Basically a chip is best played when the ball can spend most of the time running along or very close to the ground; a pitch is played when the ball needs to be kept off the ground for as long as possible. Thus, it will be obvious that a shot over a hazard (bunker, lake, pond or long and maybe wet grass) needs to be a pitch, keeping it airborne until it has safely carried the problem area.

A chip could normally be played when you have fairly flat ground between the ball and the hole, though you should be aware of the speed of the green. In some circumstances with uphill or slow greens (especially when wet) a pitch might still be the best option, landing the ball close to the pin, but that demands pinpoint accuracy. With a little refinement you can either stop the ball quickly or let it run on. We shall deal with the techniques involved shortly. Stance and grip are important in these shots as in every other, and aim is absolutely critical; if you aim off target from 20 yards (18 metres) you have no chance. That aim must, however, reflect the borrow on the green, something we shall come to soon.

CHIP-AND-RUN SHOTS

Let's begin with short chip-and-run shots and move gradually further from the hole.

With the ball on the green you would always putt, though I do remember one memorable occasion at St Andrews when José-Maria Olazábal chipped the ball across one of the huge double greens on the Old Course, to the consternation of traditionalists. He replaced the divot and was perfectly within his rights to use that shot rather than attempt a sixty-yard putt across a sloping green with a dip in the middle of it.

The best advice is to putt when you can, chip when you can't , and only pitch when you can't do either.

With the ball sitting in the fringe just off a fairly flat green, the pin some distance away, you need to look carefully at the lie of the ball. Is it sitting up? Is the grass growing against you or with you? Is the grass wet? How fast is the green? All these questions need answering in your mind before you decide which shot to play. The average higher handicap player only has one choice in most situations, partly because he lacks the experience to think through the alternatives, but better players should always have a couple of options at least.

Can you putt it? Probably not, if the fringe grass is growing against you and the ball might be snuggled down in the grass. A putt would be too dangerous. The options then, are to pitch the ball at the pin, stopping it quickly, or to chip the ball to the safety of the green and let it run. A pitch needs to be very accurate, so the latter is probably the best choice here.

Your initial thoughts must be of the slopes of the green. If you were putting, where would you aim to allow the ball to take the borrow and finish close to, or in the hole? Getting that aim right is vital. Tournament players are often seen walking the green, looking for subtle slopes that might not be obvious at first glance. As the ball slows it turns more with any slope so you really must treat this shot as a long putt, but with the first few yards of the 'putt' being in the air. In reality the ball will only get a few inches off the ground over the first couple of feet, so you must look carefully at the spot where you want it to land. That should always be on the green itself, unless the pin is very close.

From there it will react exactly like a long putt.

When practising, it is a good idea to chip the ball to various holes, marking in advance (with tee-pegs) where you want to land the ball. Ignore the hole and aim to land the ball by the tee-peg, allowing it to run. Try this with several different clubs: wedge, 9-iron, 8-, 7- and even 6-iron. The longer the club, the more the ball will run once

To play a chip shot have the ball off the back toe, the hands well ahead to deloft the club-face. It might help to grip down the club a little to restrict the wrist movement.

it lands, providing you strike it with the same length backswing, so a long chip-and-run, maybe uphill on a slow green, may be best hit with the 6- or 7-iron.

Technique

Now for the stroke itself: it is best to stand with your feet close together, very similar to your normal putting stance. Have your feet in a fairly

Don't take the club back too far or you will find that you decelerate into the ball, duffing the shot.

open position, the ball about centre or back in your stance. There should be very little lower body movement, the legs hardly moving.

The upper body stays fairly 'quiet' too, this swing being almost the same as a putt, the shoulders rocking and the arms, hands and club forming one unit.

At address the hands should be held slightly ahead of the ball and it is often a good idea to hold down the club a little extra, helping to restrict wrist movement. The weight is favouring the left side (for right-handed players).

With the ball back in the stance and the hands pushing slightly forwards, the right wrist will be very slightly bent back. Don't confuse this with cocking the wrists: in this shot they definitely do not cock and in fact stay firm throughout the shot.

With your experience in golf you should realize that flexing the knees a little to get down enough to the ball is essential, but it is worth reminding you. Most better players hit poor shots not because they don't know something, but because they have forgotten something. Have a few practice swings first, in similar length grass, to ensure you are aware of the bottom point in the swing.

The length of the backswing reflects the length of the shot and only practice will teach you how far back to swing. The important point is that the hands must be leading the clubhead at impact and then, normally, will not release but will stay firm just as on a long putt. The ball is caught slightly before the bottom of the swing so that the club centre contacts the ball. Having the hands leading will help you to achieve this. If this shot goes wrong it is normally because the player catches the ground too early. Whilst you don't want to top the ball that is preferable to catching it 'fat'.

The length of the run-out can be determined not only by the length of backswing, and thus follow-through, but by the release or otherwise of the hands.

Holding the wrists firm after impact will pull the ball up short, which is ideal on fast or downhill greens. If you want the ball to run more, going uphill or on slow greens for example, let the hands release at impact so the clubface turns over a little.

One further refinement occurs when you have the pin very close to the ball, but still have to get it airborne. You could use a very lofted club for this shot as the ball needs to stop quickly, but with little height on the ball it is difficult to get backspin. What you can do is to weaken the left hand grip, turning it more to the left, but don't alter the position of the right hand. This will prevent the clubface rotating through impact, keeping the ball on target and shorter. This is a shot which demands a lot of practice but is very effective.

To stop the ball short cut off the follow-through.

Slightly Longer Shots

As you move further from the green the shot changes in the length of the backswing, and thus the speed of the clubhead at impact. The ball should always be landed on the green wherever possible, unless the pin is very close to your side of the green when you might – but only

If you need the ball to run on, let the hands release.

73

might – land it in the fringe to kill its speed.

Always be aware of the relationship between height and distance. The higher the ball goes – normally reflected by the loft on the clubface – the less it will run on landing.

Again, the ball will stop quickly if you hold the hands firm after impact and will run on more if you release the hands.

When chipping, do ensure that you keep accelerating through the ball. If you 'quit' on the shot the ball will just jump forwards a couple of feet and stop. You must lead the clubhead through impact firmly. Finally, when chipping avoid the sand wedge. Its flatter sole makes it liable to bouncing off the ground, especially when hard, or of getting too much under the ball when sitting up, in which case the ball will stop short of the target.

THE PITCH

Now for pitching, possibly a similar length shot, but where you need to get the ball airborne to maybe carry a hazard; which might just be long or wet grass, as well as a bunker, stream, tree or something else. It is also the best shot to use if you are on a slope above the green and want the ball to stop quickly. Again be aware of the lie of the ball, for a ball sitting tight to the ground will react differently to one sitting up in fluffy grass.

There are two basic differences between a chip and a pitch: first, a chip shot is normally played like a long putt, the ball just getting airborne, whereas a pitch throws the ball high to land by the target without much run. Second, the chip shot is played with no wrist movement; the pitch is a more wristy shot.

Technique

The set-up for the pitch is similar to that for the chip shot: the feet are fairly close together, the stance slightly open to the target, the knees flexed comfortably and the ball central in the stance, a little more to the left than is the case for a chip.

Many players suggest gripping further down for this shot, but I have to disagree and advise you to hold the club as you would for any other shot, about an inch from the top. If you grip down you restrict the wrist movement, which is why you do it on a chip shot where the wrists must remain firm. Here they work the club, so you need to have them 'loose'. What you might want to do is lower your hands relative to your body, as you should in sand, in effect pushing the toe of the club slightly up. This has the effect of very slightly setting the wrists at impact, helping them to cock earlier in the backswing. You can achieve something similar by flexing your knees more, making the clubhead swing into the ball on a lower arc, getting it airborne steeper – and landing softer.

You would normally be using a very lofted club for this shot, either the wedge, sand-wedge (though not if the lie is tight or the ground very hard) or a speciality wedge, such as the sixty degree lob-wedge that I use. Obviously it depends on the length of shot.

The major problem higher handicap players have with this shot is that they try to scoop it up, letting the right hand pass the left before impact. The left hand must lead the clubhead through, hitting the ball slightly before the bottom of the arc.

The swing is fairly long yet lazy, though not to the point of quitting before impact. The follow-through will either be cut off, to kill the ball

To pitch the ball have it forward in your stance and the blade well open. Here I am using the lob-wedge.

Opposite top: The backswing should be about three-quarters at least and fairly steep. Keep still.

Opposite bottom: To hit the ball high and keep it rolling release the hands fully.

Above: To kill the ball on landing cut off the follow-through.

on landing, or released fully to allow it to run on landing. There is also more lower body movement on the follow-through than is the case with a chip, helping to keep the club going through and avoid scooping. The arms and hands are leading the clubhead at impact so it helps if the hips turn out of the way.

Choosing your landing target is vital and you should, yet again, walk to the green to look at the contours before playing the shot.

If the ball has to be hit higher, you will find that you should stand taller, which promotes a more upright swing. Bend too much and you will swing flatter, hitting the ball lower.

If the ball needs to be hit high and to stop immediately or spin back, a faster, wristier swing is required, the hands really throwing the clubhead through impact. A softer shot needs a slower tempo.

In both cases the follow-through is full, the body turning to face the target as with any other shot.

The Lob Wedge

I must also strongly advise you to consider acquiring a lob-wedge. The Mizuno wedge I use has a 60 degree loft (the sand wedge is 55 degrees, the pitching wedge 52 degrees) and is ideal for shots that need to be thrown high and stopped immediately. Hold the face as open as you can, grip at the top of the club, but lower your hands relative to your legs and take a very steep backswing, as steep as you can. The shot is a very wristy one and the clubhead is pulled to the left quickly after impact, in effect cutting off the follow-through. This is ideal when you have a bunker to carry and virtually no green to work with. To play this shot well you must be daring, but the place to see just how daring you can be is the practice ground, not the course. Perfect the art of playing this shot before you actually need it.

One thing to be aware of with this club is that, unless you are hitting out of deep rough where the ball will be difficult to control because of the grass between the club-face and ball, the ball will often stop dead once it hits the green. You need to be bold and attack the pin with this club – don't leave it short.

Most better players and nearly all professionals carry three wedges and I would urge you to do the same. After all, this is not called the scoring zone for nothing!

Downhill Pitch

On a downhill pitch stand well open and swing the club up steeply, but slowly, cutting off the follow-through. Don't quit before impact, however. If you are on a slope above the green facing a short downhill shot, always aim to land the ball on the green, never short of it. This might mean going past the pin but there is nothing wrong with that, particularly if it leaves you with an uphill putt.

Be aggressive on this shot – the more crisply you hit the ball, the better it will stop. You must lay the blade of the wedge (the lob wedge is ideal) really open and hit crisply underneath the ball. The ball will jump off the face high and will come down softly. The shot is very wristy, but the body must be held perfectly still – never move through the shot or you risk shanking it. If anything the body must be leaning very slightly back towards the right

To chip downhill you must stand very open to the target, the ball back in your stance.

foot, though be very careful to get the club under the ball.

If you are hitting downhill, aim to land the ball short of the pin.

Clip under the ball, your hands being lower than normal in relation to your body. Don't quit; make sure the ball lands on the green. The lob-wedge is perfect for this shot.

SPECIAL SITUATIONS

Uphill Pitch

With an uphill pitch you need to throw the ball high enough to land on the green close to the pin. On this, as on all short shots, aim is vital and you must take extra care in aligning the blade of the club.

Once again keep the body very still through the shot, particularly on the backswing. Depending on the distance the ball must fly you might need some leg movement through impact to drive the ball.

Always pitch the ball up to the putting surface rather than running it up the bank. Have the ball slightly forward in the stance, stand open, swing positively and throw the clubhead through impact into a full follow-through.

If there are any overhanging branches and you have to run the ball up the slope choose a spot very carefully, play the ball centrally in your stance and accelerate through impact with a fairly short back-swing. By releasing the hands at impact you will allow the ball to run more, getting over the top of the hill and onto the green.

Tight Lies

Off a tight lie, sweep the ball away as you would a putt, the club hardly touching the ground; keep your height throughout the shot, concentrating on keeping your head still. Also move the ball well back in your stance as that will help you to catch the ball before the ground. Do not use too much hand action in this shot, keeping the wrists firm just as with a putt, and don't expect the ball to stop quickly: it is more likely to run. Using a sand-wedge on this shot could be dangerous because the flange might catch the ground before you contact the ball, causing you to hit it fat, hardly moving it.

Again, I would be looking to land the ball on the green and let it run out, rather than trying to run it straight along the ground. It is a shot I practise with a variety of clubs, from the wedge to the 6-iron depending on the distance of the run-out.

Ball up against Fringe

This is a shot that is difficult to play with a putter. The best suggestion is to play the ball with a sand-wedge, deliberately 'blading' the ball (hitting it square in the middle with the leading edge of the club). Aim is vital; apart from that, play it as you would a putt, taking into account any borrow on the green. Don't take the club back too far and as you swing through make sure the blade stays on top of the grass, skimming it, rather than digging down.

Soft High Pitch

You often face a shot like this when the pin is fairly close to your side of the green and the ball is lying in semi-rough off the green. Quite often there will be a depression or slope between the ball and the green. The shot must be played from a very open stance, the ball fairly central in the stance. Use the most lofted club you have (again the lob-wedge is perfect) with the face very open and take a slow but very steep backswing, setting the wrists early. Keeping the body very still swing low under the ball – it helps to have your hands lower at address and your knees well flexed.

With the ball against the fringe it is often difficult to putt it. The best advice is to 'blade' the ball, hitting it on its equator with the tip of the sand-wedge. This will keep it running just as if you had putted it. Ensure your aim is perfect.

A full follow-through will allow the ball to run on landing; a cut-off follow-through will stop the ball. The clubhead goes through faster than the ball, which pops straight up in the air. This is the most delicate shot that you can play and is one really worth perfecting.

For a soft lob, have the ball well forward at address and swing back steeply.

Above: Throw the club under the ball – it pops straight up as you can see.

Below: Cut off the follow-through to kill the ball on the green.

9 Bunker Play

HIGHER HANDICAPPERS hate bunkers, bu if you have reached a reasonable standard you have learnt to play from sand. To be honest it's not really that difficult to get the ball out of the bunker first time, but better players want, and need, to get the ball close to the pin.

The first sensation you probably encountered with bunkers as a beginner was fear. That inherent fear in most new golfers stops them from playing well. Having moved on from the fear of failing to get the ball out of the bunker, you now need to work on getting the ball close to the pin.

The majority of players are disappointed if they hit the sand with an approach shot yet in reality if they have hit a greenside bunker at least they have hit the ball the correct distance and have hit it fairly accurately. A shot from over 100 yards (90 metres) only needs to be a few yards off-target to catch the sand so to be honest they have hit a pretty good shot. Yet they rarely see it that way. The hands go up, the head goes down. 'In the sand again!' they mutter, 'Why couldn't it have just been two yards to the right?' Well it wasn't, so the only thing to do is to learn to play bunker shots properly.

Sand Shot Technique

The sand wedge, with its heavy flange on the sole, was designed by Gene Sarazen and he became very competent with it. The sand shot demands that the clubface blasts the *sand* out rather than the ball. The sand lifts the ball out. Because of the laws of physics (which I didn't understand at school and still don't!) the ball will be blasted out in whichever direction the sand is moving. You can test this just by aiming the clubface in various directions and blasting at the sand, with no ball: watch which way the sand flies and that's the way the ball will fly out too.

This brings us neatly on to the aiming of the clubface and body.

I'm sure that for a normal greenside bunker shot you stand fairly open to the target. Most better golfers will have the clubface very open, almost pointing at the sky. This helps to get the ball airborne at a much steeper angle and obviously brings it down more steeply, stopping it better. The other main thing to remember is that the open clubface and open stance will create slice spin, so the club needs to be aimed a little *left* of the target rather than directly at it.

The backswing can cause problems to some golfers because they confuse the two targets. In every golf shot there are two target lines, the body-target line (the direction in which the shoulders are aimed) and the ball-to-target line. In the majority of instances they are parallel, though never point to the same spot. In a bunker shot the body-target line is fairly well to the left of the ball-to-target line. Yet the swing must *always* be on the body-target line, *never* on the ball-to-target line.

Because the club is lifted up apparently more steeply in the bunker shot, the temptation is to swing it down inside the line too much. That will bring it back to the impact zone too flat, risking a mis-hit. If you swing it on the *body*-target line, with the

At address have the ball slightly forward, the blade of the club well open.

clubface pointing just left of the ball-to-target line, you will hit the perfect shot.

You may need a long, slow swing, the length of your back-

A long slow backswing is often needed, though vary it according to the length of the shot.

swing and follow-through depending on the length of the shot.

If you want to stop the ball quickly on landing, stand well open and cut off the follow-through, the hands always staying ahead of the clubhead and the club-face finishing pointing directly up to the sky.

To allow the ball to run more throw the hands through impact, releasing the clubhead and completing the follow-through.

To stop the ball quickly you can also use a slightly different technique, by adopting a different grip, slightly weakening the left-hand grip. Set the club-face as open as you need for your target and as you take your left-hand grip turn it very slightly to the left, so that you have your left thumb down the centre of the shaft as you look at it. If you normally have two knuckles showing on your left-hand grip this slight alteration should make you show only one. By weakening this left-hand grip you will guarantee that the toe of the club does not pass the heel through impact. That will keep the clubface open, adding some slice spin and, adding more control in the shot. In effect what you are doing is failing to release the hands through the shot, which is correct if you want to stop the ball; the left hand will still be above the right, the back of the glove pointing almost skywards.

Varying the distance of a sand shot can also be achieved simply by adjusting how open you stand: the more open, the shorter the shot.

To land the ball softly and short, cut off the follow-through. The blade should be pointing at the sky as you finish. Stay still throughout the shot.

Although the extent of the follow-through has an effect on the distance, you must never adjust the length of the backswing; always take a full shot, accelerating the club through the impact zone. Quitting on a sand shot will just leave the ball in the sand.

You should also bear in mind the ball position in bunker shots. As you stand open to the ball it apparently moves back in your stance. Ideally it should be played from slightly forwards as the swing nadir must be under the ball in the sand. This is not a shot where the ball is hit on the downswing. If you need to get the ball high quickly, have more weight on your rear foot.

The ball position does influence the loft of the shot, so with the ball further forward you should get it higher; further back and it will stay lower.

Plugged Lies

Plugged lies are no fun and it might not be possible to control the ball once it lands on the green. The best way to play a plugged ball is to stand only very slightly open to the target, have the clubface almost square and hit down hard, almost like a punch shot from grass. Because of the lack of control on the ball you should not attempt to play a plugged ball to a tight area of green, but give yourself more margin for error. I often use an ordinary wedge for plugged lies so that the club digs down under the ball, rather than bouncing through the sand. As with every shot, you need to be positive about what you have in mind.

Wet Bunkers

Wet bunkers are also no fun and if you do encounter one make sure, first of all, that you are not standing in casual water in the bunker as you attempt the shot. If you are, you can drop the ball but only in the bunker again, so look carefully before deciding whether you might get an even worse lie.

In very wet sand with the ball sitting on top of the surface and the sand the consistency of wet cement, I would leave aside the sand-wedge and play the lob-wedge or wedge, treating it exactly like a shot from the fairway. The flange on the sand wedge bounces too much (as it does on very firm ground) and is too dangerous to use. The shot is just like an ordinary pitch, getting the ball high to carry the bunker lip and land on the green. Forget you're in sand.

Fairway Bunkers

Fairway bunkers are normally fairly easy to escape from, primarily because most of them do not have high lips at the front. Although you will normally achieve a reasonable distance from a fairway bunker never be too ambitious. Always be looking for the ideal position for the next shot, even if it means laying up from the sand. What is devastating is playing a great shot from a fairway bunker only to see it drop into a greenside bunker: don't do that. You must also avoid failing to get the ball out of the bunker if there is a high lip. In such a situation make sure the club you are using has enough loft to clear the bunker easily, even though it might mean you lose some distance. Always play sensibly.

With a flat fairway bunker and a good lie, the best thing to do is to have the ball about the centre of the stance, stand almost square and forget the idea of hitting into the

With a fairway bunker you need distance but control. With a 5-wood here I have only swung three-quarters to maintain my balance – the upper body must not sway. Do not overswing or you will lose control.

sand behind the ball. Have in mind that the ball is sitting on a sheet of glass and that you need to sweep it off cleanly. The shot is similar to that employed with a fairway wood where the clubhead comes into the ball on a very long, low approach. The vital part of this - or any bunker - shot, is to remain very still. Forget leg and lower body movement or you will mis-hit the shot. stay still, even if that means only a three-quarter swing.

Concentrating on the front of the ball rather than an inch or so behind it should help you to hit the ball before the sand. You should also have a very firm stance and grip down the club a little to ensure you don't swing the club too low.

One potential danger in trying to take the ball off the surface cleanly is that you might top it, digging it into the sand at worst, losing valuable distance at best. To avoid this ensure that the ball is no further forward than central in your stance and swing into the ball very low. On some earlier shots I have suggested you have a second, imaginary ball or target just ahead and outside the line of the real ball. In this instance imagine you have a second target 6in (15cm) ahead of the ball and an inch down into the sand.

SLOPES IN BUNKERS

Upslopes

Finally in bunkers we come to slopes. If the ball is on an upslope near the front edge of the bunker (nearest the green) the shot is relatively easy, as all you need to do is open the clubface as much as possible and really slam the club into the sand an inch below the ball, blasting it out high. It might not be possible to get too much roll on it if the pin is on the other side of the green but by releasing your hands after impact you might get a little extra distance.

Side Slopes

Side slopes are also relatively easy as you play them just as you wouldany other sloping lie. With the ball above your feet, grip down on the club and aim more to the right as the ball will hook. Be careful, however, because the loft on the clubface is decreased in this shot so the ball may race on a bit. If you have a lob-wedge use it.

With the ball below your feet, the biggest problem may be getting a good stance, as you might well have to stand (or kneel) outside the bunker. Take your time and get a really secure stance. Try to keep the lower body as still as possible; this is basically just an arms-and-shoulders shot. The stance you have will dictate whether you can aim the clubface at the target or not. If you can't, choose a safe area of green to aim at.

Downslopes

Finally the most difficult bunker shot, that from a downslope. If the ball has just trickled into the bunker it may be sitting on a downslope with the back ridge of the bunker very close. This makes the backswing difficult, for the club would normally hit the back edge, possibly taking sand (incurring a penalty!) but definitely being deflected in its path.

The first thing to consider is that this shot is going to be very difficult to

control once it hits the green, so again, choose a safe area of green to aim at, not necessarily the pin position.

Your weight will be well forward, on the left foot, your shoulders parallel to the slope, your

With a downslope stand very open to the target and set the wrists at address.

The backswing is very steep, though not full. Stay in control.

it comes up sufficiently steeply to miss the back of the bunker, yet still get the club up in something very similar to your normal bunker swing. You need to hit down very hard, very steeply into the sand behind the ball, otherwise it will not have enough momentum to clear the front of the bunker. It will also run on so if you can cut off the follow-through you might control it better.

Finally

The really important part of all bunker shots is to stay absolutely still on every bunker shot, fairway bunkers included. Do not push through with the feet or legs but stand your ground. The swing is with the arms and shoulders only and may only be a half-swing. If you move off your centre of gravity, in the backswing or downswing, you risk mis-hitting the shot.

Stay still!

stance as open as you can. Because of the angle your shoulders are at, the takeaway will appear to be steeper than it really is, getting the club up away from the rear ridge of the bunker. Do avoid trying to pick the club up too much – the angle you are standing should ensure that

10 Putting

PUTTING IS often referred to as a game within a game, which it undoubtedly is. The grip is different, the technique is different and the ball 'flight' is different.

Choosing the right putter is obviously vital; putters don't normally come as part of a set of clubs, so you buy a putter separately. Most players have more than just one and although one will undoubtedly be a favourite, most golfers tend to be a bit fickle, changing putters as soon as they start missing putts. To be honest, there's nothing much wrong with that, as putting is a game of feel.

The length of a putter can be altered just like any other club, either adding a plug or cutting off a piece of the shaft. It goes without saying that you should have one that is right for you and it is just a matter of trying them out until you feel comfortable. I am not going to comment on the broomhandle putters as I have never used one seriously. Those tournament players who use them consider them to be wonderful. If you try one and like it, then use it. Don't let anyone else play your golf game; do it your way.

The putting grip

The putting grip varies from the normal golf grip in that the forefinger of the left hand and the little finger of the right are reversed, creating the reverse overlap grip. You do see many golfers such as Langer and Faldo who are now experimenting with other grips , though I would caution against trying these unless you are desperate. If you get to that state, a visit to a teaching professional will probably do you more good than trying all the various grips and putters. Very few people have putting lessons even though putting constitutes 50 per cent of the game of golf.

Putting Technique

It has always been the custom to stand very slightly open to putt, though having said that, nowadays many tournament players are actually doing the opposite and standing in what appears to be a closed position. What you should bear in mind is that the absolutely vital part of putting is that you remain as still as possible, though without becoming rigid and losing the essential 'feel' for the stroke. Any body or leg movement in a putt is likely to cause you to miss the hole.

One other piece of advice that will help you, particularly on a long putt, is to walk to the hole and look right in it, from close up. This will reinforce in your mind that the hole is fairly large; looking at it from a distance makes it look smaller. If you are missing your putts what you do need to discover is where you are missing them; to the left, the right, or short.

CORRECTING PUTTS

Once you know what you are doing wrong you can start getting it right. Look for consistency in the missed putts. Are most of them missing to the left, or the right? If you can find a pattern you are halfway to becoming a better putter, whereas if there is no consistency to where you miss the hole you have more of a problem. Although you can only really measure your success on the golf course, rather than the practice green where you face no real pressure, do take into account the slopes on the green when looking for patterns of missed putts.

Missing Putts to the Left

If you consistently miss putts to the left the chances are that you are moving your shoulders up and to the left at impact, or you are aiming left to start with, either with the putter face or your shoulders.

Check your aim carefully, with the help of a colleague or friend. Always do this practice on a flat putting green. Get the alignment of the putter face checked carefully to see that it is aiming towards the hole. Many tour players use their caddies to help them get their aim right in tournament golf and although you probably won't have the benefit of a caddie, in a friendly game get a partner to check your aim occasionally. What you see from above the putter is not always what you would see looking down the line to the hole.

Then check that your shoulders are parallel to the ball-to-target line. This can be more difficult and again requires a colleague to help you. If you are aiming too far left, square the shoulders up, maybe standing a little closed to do so.

If your aim is good but you are still missing putts to the left you are moving your shoulders up too quickly. 'Keep your head down' is an old golf saying and it was never truer than in putting. Concentrate

You can clearly see from this picture how the left shoulder has moved up and left. The missed putt to the left was inevitable.

on keeping your head very still through the putting stroke and count to two after impact before lifting your eyes to follow the ball. You could also try flexing your knees a little more at address as that can help you to keep your head down through impact. Never putt straight-legged.

Missing Putts to the Right

In this case it is probably your aim that is off and this might be caused by the ball position relative to your feet. Check that the ball is not too far forward first of all; ideally it should be just forwards of centre of your stance, so experiment with the position until you get the ball rolling on line.

If you are happy with the ball position, look carefully at the plane of the putter swing. In an attempt to keep the putter on line you might be taking it back outside the line. In a normal golf shot that would possibly cause a slice because the putter is moving out-to-in at impact. It can happen on a putt, too, so ensure that you don't try to take the putter back too straight. It must come inside the line a fraction and holding it straight artificially will only damage your putting.

Missing Putts Short

Quite obviously the answer is to strike the ball a bit firmer – be more aggressive. Extend your arms and the putter head through the shot more, to the extent that your arms finish almost horizontal.

BETTER TECHNIQUE

The putting stroke is just a gentle rocking of the shoulders, but it is vital that the arms and wrists stay firm. Certainly the wrists are important in putting, not because they are used but because they must remain firm. If they give at all, you will either lag the putter head behind the stroke, in effect quitting on the shot, or you will flick at the ball, which is likely to send it left. Practise just rocking your shoulders to and fro, your palms held together. You don't need a putter for this.

The vital part of putting is keeping the putter head on line and accelerating through the shot. Always extend the putter head towards the hole, your wrists not breaking but remaining firm. This is important on both long and short putts. On a very short putt the putter head should finish directly over the hole.

On a very short putt have the putter head almost directly over the hole. On all other putts extend the putter towards the hole, almost steering the ball in.

catching the ball off the toe of the putter. This will slow it down and make it more controllable. It might also help if you pull your hands to the left after impact, just as you might on a sand shot that you want to kill quickly.

There are a couple of basics in putting that are often overlooked. I have mentioned the importance of staying very still throughout the stroke and that really cannot be over-emphasized. Another point is to stand tall to your putts. In the early part of this century it was the practice to be hunched over a putt; some players today are almost bent double when they putt – Langer comes to mind. However, most top teachers will recommend that you

On a fast downhill putt you might want to do something a little different and here I suggest stand comfortably upright over the putt, giving the shoulders more opportunity to rock gently back and forwards without getting out of line.

If you are a crouched putter, try standing up more, working up gradually. You will almost definitely find it helps you. Also ensure that your weight is slightly favouring the left side (for right-handers).

You must also pay attention to how you address the ball. With most shots you hold the club flat on the ground, but with a putter you will find it helps to have the toe of the putter almost touching the ground, the heel off the ground. You are, in effect, holding the putter toe down and although you might not do that now it is something you should try, as it will make a big difference to your putting. It helps to bring the putter face through square, striking the ball on the sweet spot.

The Importance of Practice

Practising your putting is something you must do if you want

You may find it better to have the heel of the putter slightly off the ground as you putt. It will ensure you hit the ball cleanly.

to improve your golf. Sadly, not enough golfers practise effectively or positively. Try the following putting practice routines.

The shoulders must rock, not turn when putting. Contrast this to the picture on page 97.

Having warmed up with a few putts to get the muscles moving, check your putter alignment; then check your shoulder alignment. Have some straight-forward putts to a hole, then place a few tee-pegs around the practice green at various distances. Putt to each of them, some long, some short. Vary them so that you never have two putts of the same length in succession. Try to have some with a degree of break rather than all flat.

Finish the routine by playing all the holes on the practice green. The aim is to get down in two every time and if you miss any hole in two, start again. This adds the pressure that you normally experience in golf.

You could also choose three holes at random, at varying distances, giving yourself both long and short putts. Play three balls to the first hole. Your aim is to sink all three balls in two shots each. If you miss, start again. Do this twice to each hole and you should have done enough.

If you are failing and becoming frustrated, stop, as no further practice that day will do you much good. You must know when to stop.

Indoor putting is something you can do as well, on a short pile carpet. Start with a long putt, getting it as far as you can, then hit the second ball just a little short, the third a bit shorter and so on. See how many you can get without going past the previous putt. Then try it the other way round, playing the first very short, the second a little longer and so on. This is very good practice for feeling the right distance in putting.

Most top professionals have almost only one thought when putting in tournaments, and that is to get the pace right. The majority of them can read greens, through experience and practice, but it is the pace of the putt that is vital. When you practise, work on the pace of the putts more than the perfect direction. On long putts in particular if the pace is right you will either be in the hole or so close to it that you can't miss the second. Getting the pace right and aiming them towards the hole (taking into account any break) will give you a reasonable percentage of successful long putts.

Perhaps the best form of putting practice is to use just your left hand and arm. In the putting stroke it is the left arm that drags the putter through the shot; the left wrist must not break down in putting. To practise the feel of this movement hold the putter in your left hand only, gripping down so that the top end of the putter grip is halfway up your forearm. Then just practise swinging the putter through the ball, extending it on towards the hole as normal. It will teach you feel. Only use this routine on relatively short putts in practice.

11 How to Win

WE ALL LIKE to win. Despite what some schoolteachers might have told you about taking part being more important than winning, it is the winners who count. Nobody remembers those who come second. At whatever level you are playing the aim is to win. There is no point trying to come second.

Although your golfing ability needs to be up to it, the art of winning is as much in the mind as in the swing. You have to be prepared to win and although you don't want to lie awake at night worrying about the next day's match, you should ensure that you are free to think about the game rather than other little problems.

For example, nothing is worse than getting to the first tee and realizing you have forgotten something. So, the evening before you play, just check your bag and make sure you have enough tees, balls, a pitchmark repairer, a couple of gloves, a clean towel. Will it rain? Is the wet gear ready? Are your shoes cleaned and dry? It might sound basic and it is, but being prepared does make a difference.

You must also remember that all golfers, at whatever standard, play in cycles, some weeks being better than others. Recognise this and don't be too concerned if you suffer a temporary loss of form. It's only natural.

Initial Strategy

Ideally you will arrive at the course with sufficient time to practise for thirty minutes or so, though circumstances and time might not allow you to prepare as you know you should. You must, though, be ready on the first tee. Are you relaxed, yet alert enough? What is the aim on your first shot? Is it your honour?

If your opponent has driven, has he hit the fairway? If so, your aim is to do the same. If he has driven into trouble your aim will be to hit the middle of the fairway. That will immediately put pressure on him and the chances are that he will fail to get out of trouble well enough to pressure you on the green. If you drive first just put it down the middle rather than worrying too much about distance.

Hitting the green in two is always a challenge on the first hole, at any level. If you play first, try to get it there, but try harder to stay out of trouble, even if this means playing short, because if you hit a bunker your opponent will feel he has an advantage. Try to get off the first green ahead or level, though don't pressure yourself if you lose the hole or drop a stroke to par. You know you can do better and you have another seventeen holes to prove it.

In matchplay in particular, always let your opponent get to the next tee first, particularly if you have won the previous hole or are leading overall. Make him wait for you, though be aware of the problems of slow play. Never be in a hurry to stride down the fairway, especially if you have hit into trouble. An anxious walk translates into an anxious golf swing.

Choosing the Right Shot

Choosing the right shot at the right time is vital, but also remember that it is no fun trying a shot that you have never played before; the place to do that is on the practice range, so if you do come across a shot that causes you trouble recreate it on the practice ground and work on it until you can play it perfectly. One of the problems with most practice ranges is that they are basically flat; when you practise you probably look for a nice flat area to play from, but how often do you get a similar lie on the course?

Only play shots you know you can play; taking risks is only for the high handicapper. If you know you can play a shot, such as hitting over a lake, carrying a cross bunker, fading the ball round trees or whatever, then play it. You might not always make it of course, and there may well be occasions when your confidence is not quite up to the shot. You might also be affected by the weather conditions. If you doubt that you can make it you probably won't, so lay up, or try something else. With trouble at the front of the green, which is where most of it is, go longer. There's nothing wrong with hitting the back of the green.

With water around a green, play safe unless you are certain of carrying it. An easy pitch is better than having to take a penalty stroke. If your pitching is good you can still save par. One other point comes to mind when hitting approach shots and that is the position of the pin in relation to the type of shot. If, for example, the pin is cut to the right of the green the best shot might be to aim at the centre of the green with a slight fade

Choose the right shot: here the safer shot is to hit long, past the flag, maybe using the banks to bring the ball back. A high shot will have more backspin.

– that way the ball will always be moving towards the pin. If you can't hit a shaped shot like that always go for the middle of the green or the safe part of it. Golf allows you two putts but you must be on the green.

If you are behind in a game, work at getting each shot as perfect as you can. Don't try to get more than one shot back at a time, unless holes are running out fast. Let your opponent make mistakes; you can't do any more.

Playing to Win

Always try to play to par, even in match-play. Forget what your opponent is taking on each hole; play against the course.

Matchplay is not so much in fashion now as it once was, which is a shame, but whether you are playing matchplay or strokeplay always be aware of where your opponent receives his strokes. Nothing is worse than playing a hole to par only to discover that your opponent, who has dropped two shots to gross, receives two shots and is level! Mark a card before you begin your round and know, going into each hole, what you have to do to win it.

COMPETITION	Monthly Medal (Matchplay).									
DATE			TIME 9-26.		COMP NO.				Handicaps	Strokes Rec'd
Player A	P. Smith								2	—
Player B	D. Jones								14	9

Marker's Score	Hole	White Yards	Par	Yellow Yards	Stroke Index	Score A	B	Nett Score	W = + L = - H = 0	Red Yards
	1	165	3	148	17					124
	2	522	5	513	⑦					452
	3	185	3	177	15					158
	4	437	4	431	①					404
	5	449	4	437	③					428
	6	482	5	477	11					420
	7	379	4	372	⑨					332
	8	415	4	404	13					383
	9	417	4	408	⑤					379
OUT		3451	36	3367						3083
	10	370	4	358	14					343
	11	502	5	494	②					429
	12	172	3	159	18					121
	13	392	4	382	⑥					358
	14	190	3	183	16					167
	15	345	4	333	12					303
	16	482	5	477	⑧					401
	17	419	4	412	④					357
	18	397	4	390	10					360
IN		3269	36	3188						2839
OUT		3451	36	3367						3080
TOTAL		6720	72	6555						5919

STABLEFORD POINTS OR PAR RESULT   **HANDICAP**

Copyright Eagle Promotions Ltd 0883 344244   **NETT**

Markers Signature ....   Players Signature ....

Mark a scorecard to remind yourself where your opponent receives strokes.

When they are losing most people take more risks, playing more ag-gressively. When they are winning they play conservatively, easing up on the gas to cruise home. In fact, you really should do the opposite. If you are behind it is because your game is not up to its normal standard, so don't take risks. Play a cautious and sensible game. If you are play-ing well and are in the lead, you can be reas-onably certain that most shots will work, so go for them. Play the spectacular shot if you know how to play it, but don't take silly risks.

Staying ahead when you are winning can be the most difficult part of golf, as many would-be champions have discovered to their cost. Knowing what you need to do to win is important, but there won't always be a scoreboard around to tell you what others are doing in a match so just play your very best. Be aware, if you can, what score (gross or net) normally wins the club champ-ionship or monthly medal. Work out in advance what you need to beat it and have a game plan, not for every hole, but for groups of three or four. Be realistic about where you might pick up a stroke to par, and where you might drop one or two. Always try to be ahead of the game.

When you are losing you shouldn't take risks but if you are winning press home the advantage. In matchplay if you are two-up, go for three to close the match out: its not wise to sit back and let your opponents gain ground on you. Kick them when they're down, otherwise they might get up and bite you! When you are winning it's because you are playing better so continue to play better and go for every shot.

Many would-be champions have started composing their victory speech, or making room in the cabinet for a trophy, halfway down the 17th. As they say in opera, it's not over until the fat lady sings, so hide your excitement, get on with your golf and don't think of anything else until the last putt goes in on the 18th. There will be plenty of time then to find space for the trophy!

It is interesting that winners always have positive images. Seve is reported to have taken several photographs of his victories around with him on tour, putting them all over his hotel room during a tournament so that, when he awoke each morning, he would feel the glow of success; he would take that glow out with him on the course.

Winners never remember failure. Jack Nicklaus was once asked if he had ever shanked the ball. 'Never', he replied, only to be reminded that someone once saw him hit a shank. 'I don't remember' was his response. That is important – winners do not remember failure.

Now for you and I it might be different. We probably don't have photographs of victories to put up around the home, but when you are on the tee, or facing a difficult shot or a crucial putt, never think of past failures. Think only of successes. It is not something you can do without training your mind and it does not happen overnight. As with physical fitness you must train yourself.

From Winning to Losing

When you are behind, play sensibly. Don't be forced into errors; don't be rushed; don't be downhearted when your opponent chips in from forty yards. Take it in your stride and just do your best. Your best won't be good enough every single day and you won't win every single game; nobody ever does. If you lose it's not necessarily because you have played poorly - it's because your opponent has played better.

What you should do is to figure out where you went wrong on any shot, then go to the practice range and work on that shot for a short time until you realize what you did wrong.

Finally, if you have just had one of those days when nothing has gone right, go home and try again tomorrow. It's only a game of golf!

12 Strategy

HAVING PERFECTED your golf shots you now need to actually play golf. There is a vast difference between hitting shots on the practice range and playing them on the course, as the situations are always different. Many people have a practice range swing and an on-course swing but better players learn to repeat the simple swing every time (well, almost!). I have discussed the art of winning; here I want to discuss the various situations on the course that will allow you the chance to beat your opponent (even if that opponent is the par of the course).

WIND

Rarely do we get those still, cloudless, perfect days; normally there is a breeze at least, more often than not a howling gale. For those who grew up on seaside links courses the wind is a constant factor and one they have, hopefully, learnt to control. The rules about playing in wind are fairly straightforward and are easily summarized in the illustration over the page.

Basically, on long shots play into the wind first, letting the wind bring the ball round to where you want it.

On short shots (from about a 7-iron down) fight the wind, so the ball holds up against it and stays straight. Playing into the wind will knock the ball down more, so you will get some stop on the green, but you must take this into account in club selection, taking *at least* one more club than you would need in calm conditions.

Playing with the wind can cause more problems than playing against it, particularly on short shots where the initial thought might be to take one club less. However, take your normal club and hit the ball higher, as though you were hitting over trees; this gets the ball up more steeply and brings it down more steeply, with less run. Hitting a ball in low with a tail-wind will make it run even more.

Most Tour professionals count the wind in extra clubs: a one-club wind, or a two-club wind. Always remember that a cross wind is 50 per cent against you so don't leave the ball short.

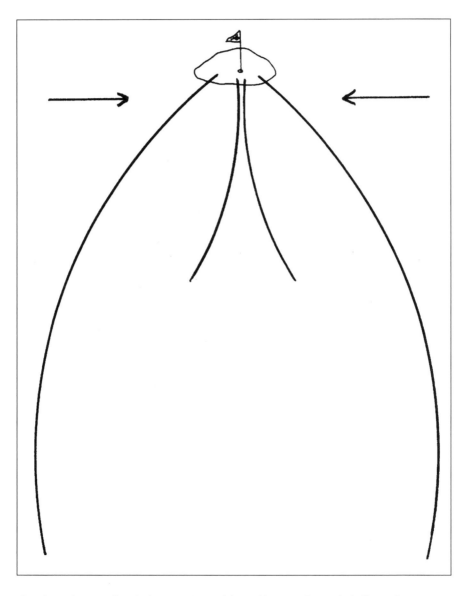

On a long shot, use the wind, aiming into it first and letting it bring the ball round. On shorter shots, fight the wind, hitting against it to control the ball better. Adjust your club selection accordingly.

SLOPES

As with wind most professionals count slopes as one more club, or they add maybe 10 per cent to the distance, so an uphill 100-yard (90-metre) shot becomes 110 yards (100 metres). The reasoning behind this is not just that gravity acts against the ball – you normally hit the ball into the air anyway and gravity pulls it down – but that the ball will hit the ground earlier in its flight uphill than on the flat. The illustration below shows this and although it is quite basic and common-sense many golfers forget it when they are playing. They get so caught up in distances that they literally forget the facts. The same goes for downhill shots. The ball is further into its flight by the time it lands so it is the landing distance that is important.

DISTANCE

I often wonder whether today's top Tour professionals could play as well if they didn't have their yardage books, or their caddies to tell them the exact distance to the flag. On the greens themselves few of us have any idea where the hole is cut unless we have passed it on

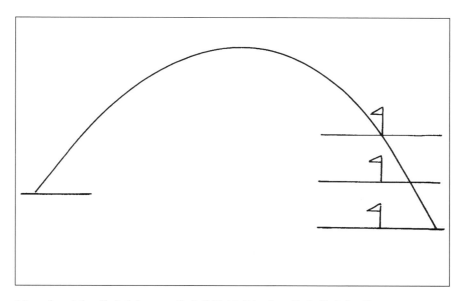

Never forget the effect of slopes on the ball flight. It is where the ball pitches that matters.

the previous hole or have good eyesight. At the level of golf you have reached you know pretty well to within a few yards how far you hit the ball with each club so you know, for example, that a 160-yard (135-metre) shot on the flat requires a 5- or 6-iron. But where do you take that measurement from, and to?

Course scorecards show the distances from the tee to the centre of the green. On some courses there

are small bushes or markers at about 150 yards (or 150 metres) from the centre of the green; in the US most courses have markings in the centre of the fairway at certain distances and professionals in tournaments have markers all over the place giving them, I sincerely believe, an unfair advantage over the rest of us.

Some golf courses have course guides, giving distances from

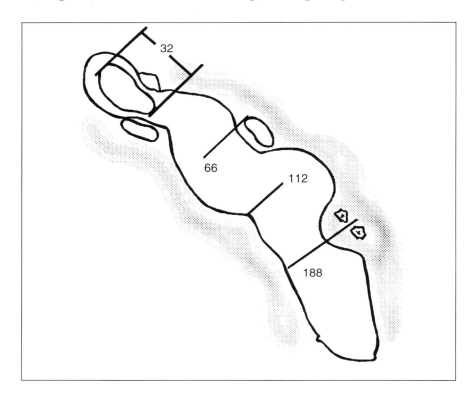

If your course has a course guide, use it!

various points to the green but in all cases you should have in mind the approximate position of the pin. If you pass a green on an earlier hole, make a mental note of where the pin is: is it front or back? Left or right? If you don't have any idea, aim for the centre of the green. The course yardage guides do normally give you the length of the green and that is important – a long green can be three or four clubs difference from front to back.

On the tee you will normally look at the scorecard for the distance but that distance is from the back cut or from the marker set into the ground. Where are you teeing from? It might be ten or twenty yards further on and although that might not be too important on a 500-yard (460 metre) par-5, it does make a big difference on a 170-yard (155-metre) par-3. Don't guess it: pace it out: know it!

On courses you play regularly you can make yourself a little course guide if there isn't one already. Pace out a few distances, particularly where you need to carry a hazard or lay up. Make notes and refer to them when you play. Get to know where the greenkeeper normally puts the pin, as they all have favourite positions.

Finally, never forget that the wind, rain and temperature affect the ball flight by up to ten per cent so your summer distances will be very different from those in December.

TYPE OF GRASS

Playing in Britain most of the year we often forget that there are other types of grass. The normal grass type in Britain is bent grass, which allows the ball to run quite well. Other countries use different grasses, primarily because of their weather. In the southern USA and in parts of southern Europe, like Spain or Portugal, the Bermuda type grasses are more common. You will notice on these that the ball will not run, so those delicate little run-up shots with the 6-iron will stop tantalisingly short of the green. Similarly the little lofted pitch from just off the green might well not work if you use your normal shot.

You must treat short shots just as you do bunker shots, hitting into the ground behind the ball and following through. You will need to hit the ball firmer (not harder) than you might in Britain. The run-up shot on Bermuda grass is not a serious option so even with a straight-in approach you need to loft the ball onto the green. The lob wedge is very effective in these conditions.

Time

We are, as golfers, always being warned to avoid the dangers of slow play. There seems, over the past few years, to have been a campaign to see who can get round the golf course in the fastest possible time. Conversely, professional tournaments are getting longer and longer with an average round of close to five hours.

The only problem with rushing round a golf course is that you will

To get an accurate understanding of the length of each hole, pace out the exact yardage on the tee. This is especially important on short par-3s.

probably rush each shot as well, rather than taking sufficient time and care over it. We all know the consequnces of rushing a shot.

Frankly, my advice is to take even more time over each shot, particularly putts on the green, for you only get one chance to get it right. Don't dawdle, of course, and don't stand around talking. Between shots move quickly to your ball and then take a minute sizing it up. Have a few practice swings until you feel happy that you have the right shape of shot in mind, re-check that you have the correct club for the distance (taking into account the wind, slope and other factors), and take another few seconds to line up properly. I can almost guarantee that this will help you to play better golf. It is interesting to watch some of the top professionals at tour events taking their time over every shot. I am not suggesting that you copy them exactly, but learn from them as they take sufficeint care over every shot. I would not knowingly hold up other players on the golf course but if people can't afford four hours maybe they should take up another sport – or spend less time in the 19th.

13 How to Practise

WHAT YOU PRACTISE rather depends on what you want to improve. In this chapter I am going to give you some practice ideas for various shots as you will only maintain your skill if you continually work at it. It is good to introduce some variety into your practice routines, either off grass at a golf course, or at a driving range, which is likely in the dark winter months. Driving range practice can be fun – you don't just have to hit the driver!

Warming Up

Any practice session (or game of golf) should begin gently, warming up the muscles first. You often see players stretching as they wait on the first tee, the club behind their back, turning one way, then the other. However, to be honest this is quite likely to cause a pulled muscle, particularly in cold weather, unless you have warmed up the muscles first.

Before you begin stretching (and this goes for either practice or a game of golf), you should increase the body temperature by 1°C. I doubt that you carry a thermometer around with you, but there is an easy way to gauge this: if you stand and very gently begin jogging on the spot, you will reach the point, probably in about a minute depending on how fit you are, where you are just beginning to perspire. At that stage you have increased your body temperature by 1°C. Easy isn't it? Now you can begin stretching.

Planning a Practice Routine

Most professionals begin their practice with the shorter clubs, using the 9-iron first for five minutes, then something like the 6-iron and so on until they are into a smooth rhythm. Then they will work on the aspect of their game that needs attention. It's not really a good idea to have more than one major area to work on in one session, though you should never work on just one club. If your aim is to improve your middle irons, work on them but also play some short and long shots to vary the routine and keep your interest level up.

The most important thing about practising is that you should have a definite object in mind and a definable method of gauging the level of your success. There are times, of course, particularly in winter, when you might not be playing too much, when you just need to swing a club to maintain rhythm and flexibility. On those occasions that's fine; just go ahead and enjoy yourself. It will help, though, once you have warmed up, to play some little games. At a driving range, for example, once you have grooved the swing into place, imagine yourself on a golf course you know and 'play' a number of holes. The first might be a long par-4 so get a good drive away, straight down the middle. That might leave you with an imaginary 4-iron to the green, requiring a slight fade. Play that shot. Imagine you miss the green short and play a pitch to the 'green' 40 yards (36 metres) away.

As well as keeping your interest this routine puts pressure on you because you only have the one shot, just as on the course. Play a variety of shots, fading some, drawing some, hitting some high and keeping others low. Always have a clearly definable target, normally the markers or flags put out at various distances. Never just hit one 300-yard (270-metre) drive after another (if only!).

Driving range practice is not perfect, but it may be the only option so make it work for you, so get some real benefit out of it.

When you are playing regularly, and can perhaps play from grass (including the practice bunker and green), you need to have definite aims in mind. Decide, before you reach the practice area or range, what you wish to practise. Be positive about it, and be precise. Warm up, run through the bag to get the swing moving nicely, then work for about twenty minutes on your chosen subject. It might be the short game to about 120 yards (110 metres). Choose a clearly definable target, a flag, a tree or, if there is nothing, stick an umbrella in the ground to give yourself a target. Hitting to empty space is pretty useless.

Gauge your success by having the balls in batches of, say, twenty. In every batch you should aim to get a pre-determined percentage realistically close to the target. It may be twelve balls in the first batch, then aim to get fifteen in the next batch and so on. This also helps put pressure on you, recreating the sort of situation you will find on the course in a match.

Never be in too much of a hurry

to hit ball after ball: take your time, wipe the club, wipe the grip, line up from behind the ball and don't always give your-self a perfect lie, notching the ball up on to a really fluffy piece of grass. Leave one or two in a divot or on a bare lie. The golf course is not perfect, either.

Try different types of shot to the target: fade one, draw one, hit one high, keep one low. Use a different club to the same distance according to the type of shot. Try to land the ball just short of the target and let it run on; then hit one high and long to land just beyond the target, hitting the back of the green in your mind. Make your practice as close as you can get to the real thing.

Ring the changes: after about twenty to thirty minutes do something different for ten minutes, like hitting some long irons, for example. Then go back to your short

Always have a very definite target. Try to play different shots to it, some with fade, some with draw, some high and some low. Learn to work the ball.

Don't always practise from perfect lies.

irons for another twenty or thirty minutes. The same applies if you are hitting drives or long irons. Only spend twenty minutes at a time on the routine, have a definite target and don't just stand there hitting balls. Move them around a little, go through your pre-shot routine. Make a habit of taking care: if you do so on the practice ground it will become second nature on the course. Also make sure you give yourself pre-set targets for accuracy. If you are working around a chipping green try to find some odd places to put the balls; a good idea is just to take a handful and throw them (making sure nobody is in the way!). Play them from exactly where they land, good lies as well as bad. Again, work to a definite target and test your accuracy.

Try different clubs for the same distance: if, for example, you have a 30-yard (27-metre) chip-and-run,

Spend half your practice time on the short game if you really want to stay sharp.

use the club you would normally use (perhaps a 9-iron) but then try something different, playing a lob-wedge to loft the ball directly at the target perhaps, and a 6-iron to run the ball in very low. Experiment: you may find some skill you didn't know you had!

Not every course has a practice bunker unfortunately and you may have to resort to asking the professional whether you can use a real bunker. I have, on occasion, used a bunker on the first green late in the evening when there are no golfers on the first hole, having obtained permission first. Whether a real bunker or a practice one, don't forget to rake it.

I also find it helpful to have some trees to hit around, under and over, as well as playing some shots from sloping lies. Most practice areas tend to be fairly flat, so again you might need to find somewhere on the course at a fairly quiet time, having obtained permission first.

Finally, go into the rough or throw some balls in among bushes or tree roots. Play them out from where they lie, even if all you can do is knock the ball twenty feet (six metres) to a clear patch of grass. Hit some back-handed, some even left-handed, and possibly a few one-handed. Try everything. You might end up in similar situations on the course and if you've never practised them you won't know how to cope. By doing this you are continually expanding your repertoire of shots, and improving your shot-making skills. When it comes down to it, the single figure golfers play better because they know how to work the ball. I remember playing nine holes once in Ireland with an octogenarian ex-professional who deliberately sent every drive into the rough so that he could practise his shots from the rough! Amazing; after all that time he was still practising.

Of course the practice range is not the only place to practise - the best place is on the course itself. If you are playing a friendly round and you have time, when you come to a difficult shot - or one that you mis-hit - drop another ball and play that as well, advising your partner beforehand, naturally. If you have tried one shape or type of shot first which has not worked as well as you would have hoped, use the second opportunity to teach yourself something. Try it slightly differently, perhaps with a different club, or hit a different shape. That is the only way to learn, by doing it. The whole idea of a practice round should be to practise, rather than worrying too much about what you score.

Putting Practice

I have already dealt with this in chapter 10 but I think it a good idea to spend some time putting on every practice session, even if only for fifteen minutes. Putting is 50 per cent of the game, so practise it.

I would never suggest you work for more than about three sessions on one subject. You must also make sure you balance what you are doing. If your main aim is the long game spend some time on the short game as well.

Finally, never practise – as in trying to improve or alter your

You can never have too much putting practice, but make sure you give yourself definite targets to help measure your improvement.

swing – before playing. Warm up by all means, working through the bag, but only to groove the swing and build your rhythm for the day; but never go to work on your game before a round of golf because you will find yourself between the devil and the deep blue sea. When you do warm up note carefully how you are playing. If you are fading the ball on the practice range you will probably fade the ball on the first tee. Take that into account and compensate. Take your practice swing onto the course with you.

If you encounter problems during the game, go to the practice ground and work on them.

Work hard on your game but keep it fun. Check the basics like aim, grip and set-up constantly. Always know what you are aiming to improve.

14 The Inner Game

IT IS OFTEN SAID that golf is 50 per cent physical and 50 per cent mental. Some might suggest the mental side counts for more but whatever you believe it is undeniable that the mental side of golf is as important as having a good swing. A number of top tour professionals use sports psychologists to enhance their game, believing that their mental abilities can be trained just like their bodies. Other players dismiss psychology as being a mere prop to lean on when things go wrong. I suppose you have to believe it might do you some good before you try it. Having worked with some psychologists it is clear that the most important part of the inner game is that you believe in what you are doing. Self-confidence in anything is vital, but can it be taught, or does it occur naturally?

Some golfers need to be really hyped up, the adrenalin flowing, before they can perform at their best; others need to be calm and placid. Looking at another sport briefly you can no doubt recall the difference between the ice-cold exterior of Björn Borg, who needed to be totally concentrated to play well, and the fiery temperament of John McEnroe, who only achieved his best when he was on the point of being violently angry. Adrenalin occurs in all of us but it needs to be channelled correctly, according to our own emotional make-up.

You might be a very calm player on the outside, showing virtually no emotion, yet you do feel emotion. If you miss an easy putt or push a drive into the rough you must be upset. How do you cope with it? A calm player will quietly smile, perhaps masking a grimace, and go and find the ball, but there must be a sinking feeling inside. How do you deal with it? Everyone is different yet the majority of golfers would berate themselves. 'You idiot! – fancy doing that!' Or, 'I'm hopeless when it comes to those three-footers.'

Straightaway this is negative and you will continue to miss three-footers or push drives out-of-bounds if you keep telling yourself that's what you *are* going to do. So, stop being critical of yourself. You know you can hit good drives, or hole easy putts, because you've done it so often in practice, or on the course the other day. You *can* do it.

You just missed that one.

If you know why you mis-hit it, and being a better golfer you are probably able to analyse your faults a little more easily than a higher handicapper, ensure that next time you double-check your grip or alignment. Whatever you do don't start fiddling with your swing, trying to change things; only do that on the practice ground.

Coping with Your Emotions

Other golfers, of course, throw a tantrum and occasionally a club, though thankfully very rarely. Several professionals, however, do throw a tantrum, either smashing their club into the ground or throwing a putter towards the bag for the caddie to pick up. You can probably think of some like that. Although this is bad manners their actions are a release for them, a safety valve to let off steam, just like McEnroe's cursing. I could not recommend you do the same, but if you are an emotional person, trying to bottle up your anger or frustration will do you more harm. What you might need to do is train yourself to express your anger some other way.

Some psychologists suggest that you should face the anger caused by the situation, but must file it away until the end of the round, or until you are on your own, maybe going to the practice ground after you finish. Then open the file and get your anger out: by all means smash a few balls as hard as you can to the end of the range. Get it out of your system. If you know you can do this at the end of the round you are giving yourself a way out of a potentially damaging situation on the course, when you need to be in control of your emotions. This does need training though, just like anything else and you won't be able to change overnight.

Concentration

One major problem we all encounter is concentration. In a four-hour round of golf you are actually over the ball (from alignment to follow-through) for about thirty minutes and you need to concentrate in chunks of about thirty seconds a time. In a social game, and normally in club competitions, you will be chatting to your partners or opponents as you walk the fairway, talking not only about golf but other matters too, such as work, family, finance, the weather, the state of the country. Then you reach the ball and you have to switch all of this off completely and concentrate for thirty seconds. You need to look at the lie, take into account the wind, the slope, any hazards, the type of shot you normally play, visualize your shot, select the club, aim, get comfortable and swing. How do you switch on concentration for those few seconds?

Again, you can teach yourself. During your daily life select, at random, an object. Concentrate on it totally for thirty seconds. Are you wearing a watch? Look at it now for thirty seconds and concentrate totally on it, forgetting even that you are reading this book. Do it now. It's difficult at first, because you still have other thoughts running around your head, but it can be learnt in time. On the golf course you will learn to treat your shots the same way. You have to close your mind to everything else.

Fear

The biggest problem in golf is fear: fear of missing the fairway; fear of hitting into the lake; fear of missing an easy putt. Having sufficient self-confidence to overcome that fear arises mainly from having done it on the practice ground. Practice does remove fear. On the course in a

difficult situation, cast your mind back to the practice ground and how you hit that type of shot time after time. You can do it. Do it now.

What happens if you miss? So what? If you put the ball in the lake, does it mean you can't afford another golf ball? If you can afford the mortgage and buy a new golf ball, where's the real damage?

As I said earlier it is only a game.

Mental Preparation

Preparation for any game of golf is important and the mental preparation is as vital as making sure your clubs are in the bag. One psychologist has the idea that you should, before a game of golf, 'play' the course in your mind, but instead of hitting perfect shots every time, hit the ball into trouble. 'Hit' it into the rough on the left of the first fairway and then visualize how you would recover from that position. By doing this for every hole you build up in your mind a repertoire of recovery shots so you become more confident when you stand on the tee in reality. Because you no longer fear hitting the ball into trouble, knowing that you can get out of it, you will end up hitting more straight shots.

There are other times when you

do hit into trouble and have what you consider an awful lie. Take a moment to walk around the ball looking at all the other worse lies the ball could have been in. It might have been right behind a tree rather than to the side of it; it might have been plugged in that bunker, not sitting up; maybe it could have rolled into the lake rather than having stopped on the edge. As in life, there is always someone worse off than you so visualize the other, worse situations you could have been in, be thankful and play the shot. It is never as bad as you thought at first.

This piece of advice is particularly relevant when you have hit a shot into trees or bushes, for my guess is that from the time you see the ball heading for the woods your head goes down and you are thinking the worst. However, wait until you get there before you get downhearted. Any 'down' in your attitude is im-mediately translated as an 'up' for your opponent. Don't give him that advantage.

Distractions

Although not so common in amateur golf, distractions are a regular feature of tournament golf and many players become rather irate at the crowd moving, cameras snapping or people coughing. Nevertheless, it is a distraction to have noises off, at any level of golf and you may well encounter some distraction yourself, be it a shout, a car horn or something else, at a critical moment in your round. If you can, stop, and start your shot preparation over from the beginning. But don't let that distraction get to you. Mentally file it away in a box along with any anger and tell yourself that you will deal with it later, after the round of golf.

The same goes for a bad shot. We all have them and those who win don't let it affect them. What they do is file that shot away, get on with the game and, only later, at the practice range, get that shot out again and work on it.

The other major distraction is people, particularly on the first tee. At almost every club you see a small group of players by the first tee waiting their turn and they can be very off-putting. Having played in several professional events I have learnt to cut them off completely but that can take some time. Most people think those watching will be critical if you mis-hit the first tee-shot. All I can suggest you do is to concentrate on your swing itself, even ignoring the fairway and just make sure that your aim is correct, and then imagine you are playing a practice shot at the driving range. Swing smoothly, but make sure you turn your shoulders fully in the backswing. Don't try to hit the ball too hard and never go for the 300-yard (260-metre) carry straight down the middle. Instead, set your mind on getting it just 200 yards (180 metres) down the middle, playing ths hot you normally play, be it a fade or a draw.

Never try anything new there and if you find you are really having probems focusing I would suggest you use a 3-wood rather than the driver.

Whilst being polite and pleasant to your fellow golfers – several of whom may be good friends – as soon as you are on that first tee (or any other tee) totally ignore everyone and just concentrate on yourself. It does take some time to achieve this but you should start it now, not on the first tee but on any hole when you are over a particular shot and your playing partners are around you. Turn them off completely for the thirty seconds it takes you to align yourself and prepare to swing the club.

Finally, always remember that, as a single-figure golfer you have a responsibility to less accomplished players. Be considerate, be polite and be helpful to all you meet. Give advice if asked to and get to know the rules – other players will look up to you. Make surethat you are worthy of their respect.